A Journey of Challenge, Commitment and Reward

Tales of a City/County Manager

James M. Bourey

This book is dedicated to the thousands of local government managers who work so very hard and selflessly to improve the quality of our communities and their families that support them and enable them to do what they do each day

ISBN 978-1-7350811-1-3

Acknowledgements

It is not possible in this acknowledgements to recognize the countless number of people who have contributed to the successes of the places I worked as well as provided me invaluable guidance along my professional and life journey. As with most authors, nothing of who I am and the path I followed would have been possible without my parents. Aside from the obvious conception and birthing part, I am always amazed at the incredible influence parents have on their sons and daughters' motivation, values and moral compass. I could not have had better direction in all these aspects of my character. Who I have become and anything positive I have contributed along the way grew from the love and guidance of my parents.

My eternal gratitude goes to my wife, Ann, who has been a constant source of love and support for the 43 years we have been together. The reader will learn more about the tremendous assistance that Ann has contributed throughout my career and life for our decades together. In addition, Ann provided invaluable editing to help correct errors and make the book more readable. My daughters, Jennifer and Christine, have also given immeasurable love and support throughout this journey. Their understanding and patience was critical as we made many stops along the way.

My brother, Alan, also has provided great support throughout my life and professional career and added his insight for the writing of this book. It is hard to explain to others the bond that identical twins have. People often ask me what it is like to be a twin. My response is generally, to ask them what it is like not to be a twin. It is all I know. I do know I would not trade it for the world!

I am grateful to a number of professional city/county managers who read versions of this book and made insightful comments. These are people that I warmly regard as friends and their thoughts and suggestions contributed to making this a better book. Thank you Gary Jackson, Robert Hyatt, Ian Kaiser and Dave Childs.

In addition to providing input on writing this book, I am most indebted to Dave Childs for his an insightful and wonderful forward for this book. Dave has been a good friend since our days of working in Minnesota. We met when I was attempting to repair some of the relationships between the Hennepin County where I was managing and the cities in that county which included the City of Minnetonka, which he was managing at the time. My wife and I have valued the friendship with Dave and his wife, Barb.

There are so many former bosses, staff members, mayors and council members who played such an important role in the successes of places I worked. I will refrain from mentioning them here but many are included in the book itself. I was but one of so many people who worked to make all those places as wonderful as they could be.

Contents

Contents..6

Foreword 8

Introduction...13

Summary Resume...18

Chapter One..21

Being a Manager: Big Challenges and Big Rewards

Chapter Two 48

A Variety of Forms of Local Governance

Chapter Three...61

The Path to be a Local Government Manager

Chapter Four...66

Leadership Qualities

Chapter Five..78

The Job Search Process

Chapter Six..98

Navigating the Minefield

Chapter Seven 113

Organizational Growth and Change

Chapter Eight..125

Community Involvement is Critical

Chapter Nine...136

Dealing with the Media

Chapter Ten 147

The Hiring Process

Chapter Eleven 154

It's About We not Me

Chapter Twelve.. 162

Public Private Partnerships

Chapter Thirteen 182

Big Risk, Big reward; How Much Risk is Appropriate

Chapter Fourteen 194

Successful Downtown Development

Chapter Fifteen.. 208

Emotional Intelligence

Chapter Sixteen 215

Outcome Based Performance Measurement

Chapter Seventeen 220

Departing Gracefully

Chapter Eighteen.. 229

Transitioning to the Private Sector, the Not So Dark Side

Chapter Nineteen 234

So What is Next for You and for Me

Foreword

By Dave Childs, ICMA-CM

Past President of ICMA

Whether you're an aspiring local government manager or a seasoned professional it's true that all of us can benefit from great stories that help us understand and frame the world in a better and more understandable way. In this book, Jim Bourey tells stories about his long and successful career as a local government professional. And, as you are about to see, there are real insights and deep meaning to be taken from Jim's writings.

Reading stories about working in the trenches of local government management can provide us with a framework for viewing the situations that we will inevitably encounter in our careers and, more importantly, guidance in how we should use our knowledge and skills to manage those situations. Or, for the more experienced practitioner, we may find it helpful in reaffirming our approach or charting course corrections in our career based on new and valuable insights.

Over the years, I have been blessed to sit with groups of seasoned managers who are gathered around the table telling story after story on into the evening. Many of the tales are funny, some are thoughtful and moving, and some are just plain unbelievable. In my experience, most of the unbelievable stories are true, and the funny stories may turn out to be just as sad as they are funny. And, in the end, it turns out that the thoughtful stories are much more than that. Often those thoughtful stories are amazingly profound and powerful. Underneath, they are stories of courage, and principle and grit...and even of love. In the telling they reveal what is so compelling and moving about the "calling" that is local government management.

But it's more than stories, isn't it? Writing a book about one's career sprinkled with stories that are sad, funny, thoughtful and amazing is really just the start. Jim delivers much more in this book. He delivers the things you will need in order to truly understand the triumphs and the challenges of being a local government manager.

I believe that Jim Bourey has found a way to give you maximum value from this reading by providing you with three key things, beyond the stories, that you can take away with you.

First of all, these stories, tales and anecdotes need to be firmly grounded in certain **principles**. Whether they are management principles, principles of human relations, principles of leadership, or whether they are key ethical principles, this is where we ground ourselves as we move forward in our daily work. Jim helps us to understand these principles and then, secondly, he demonstrates **why** these principles and these stories truly matter, and **why** all of the things that have come together in Jim Bourey's career and in his life have made a difference in the communities where he has served. And **why** his efforts and those of his colleagues have enriched the lives of the people who live in those communities. Third and most importantly, however, we need to be able to take away the clear **insights** that flow when stories are tied to principles. We need the context, the "why" and the "principles" all wrapped up in great stories to ultimately be able to form those keen "insights" so necessary to pull it all together. Jim has written a fascinating and compelling book and I am sure that you will enjoy the journey with him in the coming pages.

Stories, principles and insights. That's what you will get in "A Journey of Challenge, Commitment and Reward".

Jim thoughtfully weaves the tale of his career, his life and his family with his chosen calling...serving the public. I met Jim back in the 1990s when I was the City Manager of the City of Minnetonka, Minnesota (in Hennepin County) and he had just become the Hennepin County Administrator. We hit it off right away and worked together on key projects and issues. Our friendship has continued over the years as our careers have taken us around the country. I retired a few years back after 43 years in local government and having had the honor of serving as the President of the International City/County Management Association during my career. It's been a great ride and Jim has been an amazing colleague and friend.

Both of us use the word "calling" when we refer to our work because it is truly a career of public "service" and something that truly comes from the heart. Now that I'm one of the grey-haired oldsters I love to tell the tales, too. Stories of environmental disasters, floods, tornadoes, financial collapse, and citizens and employees who do and say stupid things. And of course, I also love to tell the stories about what I call my "career days". Those are the days when two or three great things happened in a way that you felt enormous satisfaction as you walked out of the office door at the end of the day. "Career day" moments like when an employee comes by your desk to say that because of the work we have been doing to improve our organizational culture they now love to come to work every day because it's the best job they ever had. Or when a citizen tells a heartfelt story at a public meeting about one of your employees who went far beyond the call of duty to solve a problem. Or when the citizen satisfaction survey comes back and the numbers are the highest ever. Career days...those days when things are going right and it's not about "me" ...it's about making a difference for "them". That's why this work is truly a calling.

So, here's one of my stories (with a principle and hopefully an insight for you to take away with you.)

A few years back, I was driving on the freeway in the Minneapolis/St. Paul area, where I had been a City Manager in three different cities over a period of nearly 20 years. As we went through the City of Minnetonka on the freeway, I said to my wife, Barb, "Hey sweetie, we're driving through my little town!" To which she replied, "Honey, you've been gone for 5 years, this isn't your little town anymore."

On we drove and soon we were passing through City of New Brighton, where I had been the City Manager before I went to Minnetonka. And I said excitedly, "Hey sweetie, we're going through another one of my little towns!" And, Barb predictably responded, "No Dave, this one isn't your little town anymore either".

A short while later we were going through the City of St. Anthony where I had been the City Manager before I went to New Brighton and yes, once again I said, "Hey sweetie, we're going through another of my little towns". And my dear wife, as only she can do, said to me, "You moron, this isn't your little town anymore."

Well, here's the thing. These will ALWAYS be my little towns. As local government managers, we don't just show up and "manage things and people", we pour our hearts and souls into our communities every day. These communities become our home and a place that we love. And yes, we may leave for a job in another "little town" (sometimes voluntarily, sometimes not) but I can say without a doubt that when we leave, we each leave a big piece of our heart behind. Every. Single. Time.

And every single time we try to leave our little town better than we found it.

Because, in the end, "they won't care how much you know until they know how much you care."

Read that last sentence again, because that's the meaning that we derive from the work we do and that's why it truly is a calling.

Yes, stories help us frame our work as local government managers and **why** it is so important. Stories help us understand the **principles** that apply to the work that we do. And, in the careful telling, they provide us with the **insights** that we can use as we chart our own course in our lives and careers. Enjoy Jim's tales and insights! You won't be disappointed.

Introduction

I invite you to share my journey, a journey of compassion, commitment and unending challenge. It has not always been an easy journey, but it has provided a great sense of reward. This is a deeply personal story about not only the profession of local government management but also about its interplay with life. This journey of my career is offered to be helpful for people who are on the same road or considering it, who have been on similar journeys, who have been along with a loved one as they traveled the path and yet others who may just be curious. I expect the seasoned manager will read with a feeling of familiarity; sometimes filled with a sense of pride for the profession or often understanding the struggles along the road; frequently wearing a knowing smile or frown, but most often with a knowledge of the fulfillment that public service provides and a deep awareness of the demands that journey held for them and their family.

I fully expect that the longtime manager may not always agree with my perspective. Dialogs with differences in perspective can enrich the profession. Those that may be new to the profession or are in mid-career will likely be both excited and apprehensive. My hope is that those that made the journey along with a husband, wife, father or mother who was a manager, will have a sense a pride for the accomplishments of their loved one but I also know they will have experienced some of the tough times that can accompany a manager's service. I hope the curious reader gains a knowledge of the profession, the sacrifices that are made, but, most importantly, the wonderful reward the profession brings to those who commit themselves to helping communities be their best and the tremendous value of public service.

I have really good news to those readers that bought this book to get all the answers for how to be a successful manager. You are only in the third paragraph and hopefully you have not creased the spine and can return the book, so you can avoid disappointment. If you want to explore a most noble calling with a long time practicing professional, then, take a chance and keep the book. I truly hope, if you read on, you will find the lessons included interesting and helpful. Neither I nor anyone else has all the answers; however, by sharing this story, I hope to contribute to the profession. For several years before writing this, I asked myself the very hard question; with all that has been written about local government management, will what I have to say contribute to the profession. I have not seen books that tell a personal story in a way that brings out the lessons learned along the way. At the end of reading this, I hope you will agree the message has value.

This book is not a textbook on the practice of local government management. Nor does it provide complete instructions on how a manager should operate. In fact, as I mentioned, some may disagree with my perspective as it sometimes challenges the traditional view of a manager's role. While this is a true account and I have attempted to fully describe the setting of each story, I have sometimes omitted names or confidential parts to avoid embarrassing people. It does include some situations where I have signed separation agreements which prohibit me from disclosing details or being critical.

The book provides a perspective on the professional challenges as well as approaches to handling important issues and public policy. It provides an insight into the life of a local government manager that is introspective and unvarnished, as hard as that can be at times. The book is personal because our profession requires a personal commitment and, I think, you must really care deeply for people and communities. We may work in many locations during a career, as I certainly have, but you must commit yourself to each of the locations you work and truly want to make it the best place possible.

The organizations I have managed have had many successes; however, these were successes for the organization not just personally mine. I do fear that the reader may get the impression that I think the stories are all about me, but they include all those people that I worked with along the way. Of course, I hope I did play a role in those successes. I have experienced many challenges, especially with city councils. Reading this book may help you avoid learning some lessons the hard way. I have done a lot of training in emotional intelligence and will describe in a chapter the programs I helped to establish in several locations. In 2001 I co-authored an article with Athena Miller (more about her later) about one such program for *Public Management Magazine* and will not forget a letter written by a manager to the magazine that said if he had read the article six months earlier, he might still be employed. I do think there will be value for practitioners. Hopefully, the book will help people be successful in charting their course. I have had a strong commitment to make a difference and feel I have done so. Many have said I made a big difference, others may undoubtedly disagree with that assessment. I will leave that judgment to others.

Maybe "The Natural" exists in sports or other pursuits but nothing comes without work and, at times, struggle. Tiger Woods, Tom Brady and Michael Jordan may be gifted athletes, but they did not reach the mountain top of their sports without a tremendous amount of practice. But even people who are not gifted athletically can be the best at what they do. Larry Bird is not considered a great athlete, but he was amazingly successful as a basketball player, a sport that few would argue has some of the best athletes in the world.

This book explores a wide spectrum of the personal and professional dimensions of being a local government manager. It includes a perspective on preparing for the job, the qualities of an excellent leader, searching for and successfully competing for positions and council-manager relationships, in addition to handling the media, hiring great people, risk taking, the best way to leave a position and making the transition to a different role, including moving to the private sector. It also delves into the forms of local governance, community engagement and development as well as organizational growth and change. Of course, a full exploration of each of these areas would require its own book and indeed, books have been written about each of these topics. Rather, this book attempts to add to what has already been written and what professionals commonly study in public administration classes. It focuses on lessons learned along the journey of a practitioner. I hope that many will agree with the perspectives provided; however, it is certain that some will have a different viewpoint. The writing will be worth it if those that disagree are encouraged to think through their views and carefully consider their best path forward. The most any local government should ask is for commitment, compassion and always doing your best to assist your community.

The reader will see that the book is organized around topics relevant for city management not chronologically with my career. That is because this needed to be about the lessons learned and not focused on my career. In addition, there are stories from different positions that are relevant for individual topics. So, in order to assist the reader in understand the sequence of my career, I am including a summary resume after this introduction. The first chapter provides a view into the life of a city/county manager as well as how and why I ended up on this career journey.

JAMES MICHAEL BOUREY

Education

Bachelor of Environmental Design, 1974
North Carolina State University, Raleigh, North Carolina

Master of Urban Design, 1976
Washington University, St. Louis, Missouri

Master of Architecture, 1976
Washington University, St. Louis, Missouri

Employment

Senior Community Planner, 1977-1979
Metropolitan Planning Commission
Nashville & Davidson County, Nashville, Tennessee

Manager, Physical Planning and Design Section, 1979-1982
City of Tulsa, Tulsa, Oklahoma

Director, Department of Community Development, 1982-1985
Cherry Hill Township, Cherry Hill, New Jersey

Director - Office of Planning, 1985-1987
City of Seattle, Seattle, Washington

Senior Assistant County Administrator, 1987-1993
Hillsborough County, Tampa, Florida

County Administrator, 1993-1996
Hennepin County, Minneapolis, Minnesota

Executive Director, 1997-2003
Maricopa Association of Governments, Phoenix, Arizona

Chief Administrative Officer, 2003
El Dorado County, Placerville, California

City Manager, 2004-2010
City of Greenville, Greenville, South Carolina

Director of Corporate Development, 2010-2013
Elliott Davis, LLC, Greenville, SC

City Manager, 2013-2017
City of Newport News, Virginia

Director, Management Services, 2017-2019
McGill Associates, Raleigh, North Carolina

President, Bourey Consulting, 2019-Present
Lake Forest Park, Washington

Professional Affiliations

Life Member, International City-County Management Association

Washington Local Government Management Association

Life Member, American Planning Association

American Planning Association, Washington Chapter

Urban Land Institute

Chapter One

Being a Manager: Big Challenges and Big Rewards

For the entry level professional: So, you really want to be a city/county manager?

For the seasoned professional: Are you happy you devoted yourself to be a city/county manager?

For the curious: What the heck is it like to be a city/county Manager?

For those that may have some idea of the challenges a city/county manager faces: Why would anyone want to do this?

This chapter will focus on the experience of being a local government manager. There are certainly many great options for public service. Every day, people make valuable contributions working for the federal, state, regional and local governments. On the local level itself, there are a multitude of avenues of service. Coming out of graduate school, my goal was to be the planning director of a relatively major US city. I achieved that goal relatively early in my career and ended up spending 25 years as a local government manager. While there are so many ways to make an important difference, this book focuses on being a local government chief executive. After reading, some may decide being a manager is awesome and some may conclude it is not for them. Many of the curious readers may be inspired and develop a great appreciation for managers and yet others may scratch their heads and wonder why people would do such a thing.

Path to be a manager

Later, a chapter is included on the various pathways to become a local government manager, but I want to focus on why that ended up as my life's work, some personal aspects of my life that have made a difference in the professional journey and the experience of being a manager. This needs to start from the beginning, I mean the very beginning. I am an identical twin; I have all kinds of great stories that go along with being a twin, and there are indeed some mysterious things that I do not think my brother, Alan, or I can explain.

One aspect of our experience is particularly salient for this story. While we are identical, we are also mirror images. Although, some mirror image twins actually have their hearts on different sides, we both have hearts on the left side. I am left handed and he is right handed. While we are so very much alike, what differences that do exist follows the literature of left vs right brain dominance. Of course, I love to say that he is not in his right brain (and I, a left hander, am in my right brain). It is interesting that he went into law and has had a long career as an attorney and I ended up going to the School of Design at North Carolina State University where half the students were left handed, way above the representation in the general population. And to confirm for you that Alan is not in his right brain, he went to the University of North Carolina. Alas, the very spirited rivalry resulting from our choices of colleges has mellowed greatly over the years!

Alan and I hiked the Canyon "rim to rim" in the year of our 60th birthday to celebrate together. The approximately 24 mile hike took us 13 hours.

Alan and I at the edge of the canyon

The Grand Canyon has spectacular views from many vantage points. The canyon floor is over a mile lower than the North Rim. It is almost that much of an elevation gain back up to the South Rim. It was about 40

23

degrees at the start of our hike and well over 100 degrees at the bottom of the canyon.

Grand Canyon from the North Rim

I was indeed one of those kids that could not get enough of Lincoln Logs and those plastic toy interlocking building blocks (before Legos). I loved to create buildings and places and from a relatively early age wanted to be an architect. I wanted to create places for people to live in and enjoy. I wanted to create an experience that would enrich their lives.

While so many aspects of my initial architectural studies resonated with me, my skill level with drawing and documenting what I was able visualize in three-dimensional space could have been stronger. And to me what happened in the larger context of cities and urban spaces was more exciting than individual buildings. This pushed me to be an urban designer and planner. But there was so much more to the environment than the physical buildings and spaces created, it was also about how people used the space and their experiences in the space.

I love going to cities in various parts of the world and experiencing the environment and how people use it. As I wander through cities, I love to just absorb everything that is before me and experience the place and better understand the lives people lead or did lead many years ago when the place was originally created. Throughout the world, especially in older European cities, there are great urban spaces that serve as the lifeblood for human interaction and commerce. These are places of great celebration, wonderful food and enjoyment. There are also special places for relaxation, contemplation and self-renewal. Yet other places provide surprise, delight and discovery.

One of my absolute favorite cities is Venice where canals and boats dominate instead of roads and automobiles. I love to just wander through the narrow walkways experiencing the amazing spaces and get lost in the labyrinth of passageways and canals, all the time absorbing the richness of the materials and textures of the buildings as well as the walkways and vegetation which brings a softening and vibrancy to the environs. Helping cities to develop a rich urban environment has always been a motivating force in my work.

In addition to the design of cities, I have always been fascinated by the infrastructure that provides the services which allow cities to function. The water, sewer, storm drainage and transportation systems form the backbone of our urban areas. Just as our body's skeletal system, veins and arteries, spinal cord and extensive system of nerves and digestive tract are essential to human life, public infrastructure gives life to our cities. Just as we can take for granted our internal body systems until something goes wrong, people also tend to take for granted our physical infrastructure

An alleyway in Dubrovnik

View of a canal scene in Venice

until there is a sewer backup, a storm drain is not adequate to handle a heavy rainfall, a drought limits our water consumption or we sit in traffic as our transportation system becomes congested.

As enthralling as the physical environment was, my interests went beyond those considerations. Especially while in graduate school, I was fascinated with the economic and social fabric of cities, how they grow and what makes them prosper. I did coursework in many of the terrific graduate programs at Washington University, including Business, Law, Economics, Urban Studies and Political Science as well as Architecture and

27

Urban Design. My graduate thesis was a study and the development of a theory of how land uses are allocated in cities through our economic, legal and governmental structure. In seeking to fully understand this process, I believed I could be more effective in improving conditions in cities for people.

So, not only did I aspire to help make spaces that people enjoyed and ensure adequate public infrastructure but also wanted to help the social and economic environment. Providing a thriving economic climate with good jobs and a rich social fabric were as important to me as creating a wonderful physical environment. Granted, that is a lot to take in but it has driven a lifetime professional commitment for me.

Another very critical part of the driving force behind my career choice developed as I moved into being a supervisor and gained more responsibility as a manager. The tendency towards being a bit shy gave way to a joy of working with people and helping them be successful at their tasks. What can be so darn challenging in guiding people is even more rewarding with their success. My experience is that people want to make a difference and be successful at what they do. The pleasure they experience at accomplishing their objectives, is a great reward for a manager. To me, it is like an intoxicant, once you experience it you want more and more of it. These driving forces are important for understanding the tremendous sense of satisfaction my career has provided.

There are some other aspects of my life that will also give the reader an insight to my drive and willingness to take on most any challenge. We all have some things in our lives that have put us to the test. One of mine has been periodic back issues. In high school, I injured my back working out for wrestling my senior year. I was not as careful as I should have been lifting weights and ended up with a ruptured disc and surgery during the Christmas season. I did get to be home for Christmas day. Fortunately, the surgery was a great success and I had no issues until I hurt it again playing basketball during my final year of graduate school. Due to health insurance issues, I did not have the problem addressed until I was a three months into my first job. While this was very painful, it is hard for me to regret this second injury as I had this lovely physical therapist. Although she did not resolve the problem and I had to have a second surgery, I was smitten enough to spend, so far, the next 43 years with her. We got married in 1978 and it was the most brilliant decision I have probably made. Yes, she has been helpful as a live in PT, but, more importantly, she has been a life partner whose support has been immeasurable. You will hear much more about Ann in this story!

I did have some bouts of back issues, but they subsided over time and the back held up through a lot of physical activity. However, I injured it yet again in 2018 and had a third surgery. I am back to an active lifestyle with not much restriction.

We all have heard the adage, what does not kill you will make you stronger. I am not so sure that is terribly true and is certainly not always the case. However, I think my will to recover and overcome adversity is very strong. That will was tested again in 1983 and my wife's great support and her fortitude was so important for our family. I woke up one weekend morning with a rather severe earache. We went to an urgent care facility and it was diagnosed as a middle ear infection. The next day, I was very dizzy. A second doctor's opinion was that it must be an inner ear infection. The next day, I lost control of the facial muscles on the left side of my face. My wife and I were mystified as to the cause.

I went into the hospital and spent five days very ill with a headache, dizziness and vertigo. After the telltale sign of shingles appeared by my ear, they were able to diagnose that I had shingles in the cranial nerves in the left side of my head. This is referred to as Ramsay Hunt Syndrome. It is quite rare. They really could not give us a great idea of the prognosis. Ann was working part time and attending graduate school at Temple University in North Philadelphia. Our oldest daughter, Jennifer, was two years old and Ann was seven months pregnant with our second child.

There is never a good time for something like Ramsay Hunt to strike but this was most disconcerting.

I returned home not much improved, but they had done all they could do to help. Now there is medicine that can treat shingles, but not at that time. While still not feeling well, I just felt that I needed to push myself to get up and start the recovery process. I remember my first steps outside with Ann supporting me for a short walk. When our second daughter, Christine, was born I was able to walk the halls of the hospital much of the night with my wife as we were trying to encourage her labor to progress. My daily walks became longer and stronger and within six months I was back to running. However, it took a couple of years to get over the dizziness issues, and, in particular, the vertigo when I moved my head from side to side.

I credit the great support from my wife and a ton of determination to come back from Ramsay Hunt as well as the back injuries. I tell these stories because that level of determination has been critical throughout my career journey. One of my department directors once told me I was one of the most resilient people he had ever met.

Alan and I hiked a portion of the Appalachian Trail to celebrate turning 65. At the time I had been experiencing some leg pain that turned out to be the beginning of a problem that led to my third surgery. However, nothing was going to prevent me from joining my brother for our time to celebrate another milestone birthday. The first day we limited ourselves to 15 miles which I did on crutches. As you might imagine that was quite a conversation starter when we came across people on the trail. After the first day, I graduated to some hiking poles and we upped the mileage to about 20 miles per day. Had I mentioned being determined?

Alan and I on the Appalachian Trail (Alan in on the right)

Professional choices and life experiences

Those embarking on a city/county Manager career do need to ask themselves some very important questions:

What do I want from life?

What do I want for my family?

How much am I willing to move?

How many hours a week am I willing to work?

What type of community do I want to live in?

Do I want to devote myself to being a great technician or do I want to be engaged with a wide variety of disciplines?

Am I willing to lead a very public life?

What difference do I want to make in a community?

We could go on and on with such questions, but you probably get the idea. This chapter is not meant to be discouraging but rather a wake-up call. In fact, while the journey was often a difficult one, I believe in the Satchel Page adage to "never look back!" How much of that is because I cannot change the past or because I am happy with how it all turned out, I do ask myself. However, I *always* reflect with a sense of wonder and accomplishment on my professional experiences and the successes I was a part of in the communities where I worked. But I also think about the life my family led. While my daughters grew up to be amazing people, smart, confident and caring, wanting to make a difference in the world; would they have been better off without the moving and a Dad less engaged with work? My wife was always incredibly supportive, but I know it was not always an easy road for her. Without question, I could never have accomplished whatever I have in my career but for my family. They were my rock in a world that was not always easy to navigate. They were a motivation to succeed. Their belief in the value of what I did helped to sustain my commitment to make a difference every day. This was not something we talked about and my family may even be a bit surprised to read this. But their love and support made the journey possible and meaningful.

Manager's lives are far from all alike. I have manager friends that spent most, and sometimes all, their careers in one community. For instance, one of my manager friends, Greg Kelly, after some time as a private sector attorney, spent his entire public service career as a Town Attorney and

Town Manager with Abingdon, Virginia. I have not done a survey but believe that those who have stayed in one location are a relatively small minority of professionals. On the other end of the spectrum, some managers have moved quite a bit and served many communities.

My career took me to 10 cities in ten different states. Including my childhood years, I have lived in 16 states and 30 cities. With my semi-retirement and move to the west coast, my wife and I have moved a total of 20,000 miles, all within this country, in our shared life together. My colleagues have sometimes said it would be easier for me to tell folks the states I have not lived in. Even though I often say that "move" is a four-letter word in our household, I also know the incredible richness our experience has brought to our lives. While there are so many things that are common to the different parts of our country, we have developed an appreciation for the cultural treasures of each state or region. We have lived in the Northeast, Southeast, Midwest, Southwest and Northwest and have visited all 50 states. After fully immersing ourselves in each of these regions, we were confident in our decision to move to the Seattle area where we expect to be for the remainder of our lives.

If it was not obvious, I am indeed married to an angel who has always been so tremendously supportive. Fortunately, her career as a physical therapist not only gave us more flexibility for where we lived but also allowed her the opportunity to do so many things that made it more feasible for me to work the 60 to 70 hours a week and more I did throughout most of my career.

In addition to providing that support at home my wife, Ann, was an asset in the communities where I have worked, and we have made home. While Ann is naturally not extremely outgoing, she learned to be comfortable in public settings and at all sorts of public events. She also participated on her own in the community and made a difference in some important ways. I find that communities not only like to know who their manager is but also know the values they hold and their personal commitments. By meeting Ann and getting to know her they got a great insight into the person who was managing the City. It was always a package deal.

Certainly, very few managers have logged 20,000 miles of moving but many have lived in numerous communities. While working in a number of places, some have still spent their entire careers in the same state. I have found this to be especially the case in North Carolina, a great state for city and county managers. For instance, many North Carolina managers will know Robert Hyatt, a terrific city and county manager, who worked in a number of places in the state, including serving 17 years as the Davidson County Manager.

Mount Rainer is visible from Seattle 93 miles away on a clear day

Butchart Gardens in Victoria, British Columbia, a ferry ride away from Seattle, was created out of an old quarry

The challenge of moving gets a lot more complex trying to balance a manager's career with a life partner's career. While it certainly was not always easy for my wife as she left more than one job that she really liked, we were very fortunate. I used to say, without kidding, that as a physical therapist she could get a job within 24 hours of us moving to a new place. Of course, getting a PT license in all those states was a chore. Many other managers are much less fortunate, and one really must reflect on the need to be equitable with your partner in considering relocation.

Obviously, moving can be tough on children. We made three moves when our daughters were in school. The toughest was when Jennifer was in high school and Christine in middle school. However, just as my wife and I were enriched by our experiences, there were significant benefits for our daughters. Not that they would not have been self-confident women, but I think they would agree that moving helped to give them added skill and comfort in adapting to new settings, meeting people and adjusting to new situations. I am not so sure Christine would have been comfortable enough at 19 to travel by herself to Katmandu, Nepal to work for the summer and follow that up with many trips to India and Africa as well as other countries. Jennifer has also travelled extensively, and my wife and I have also been self-assured in visiting different parts of the world and 25 countries.

Santorini, one of the many Greek Isles Ann and I visited on a cruise of the Mediterranean

Market area in Dubrovnik, Croatia

While transitioning from one place to another is never easy, I feel that it is easier than it was prior to modern communication technology. The more seasoned managers will remember the time when everyone did not have a mobile phone and anyone in the world was not just a touch of a keypad away. This may stretch the imagination of the younger reader. Back more than 30 years ago, our family made the transition from the Philadelphia area to Seattle. That was the last move that I paid for; after that, I swore I would not relocate without the city, county or company paying for it. As usual, I ran the upfront scouting party, starting work two months before my family arrived. The 3,000 mile drive across the country was a bit long but a fascinating experience. Everyone should do it once; of course, we ended up doing it more than once. Since I was only going to be in a temporary rental for a couple of months, I did not want to incur the significant, at least to us at the time, fees for installing phone service, aka, a landline for the younger reader. So, it was a pay phone down the hall that was my only communication device with my wife when our 20-month-old daughter fell off a slide and my wife was on watch that night for any symptoms of a head injury. How incredibly helpless I felt 3,000 miles away and not knowing what was happening.

Moving from one area of the country to another has necessitated adjusting to interesting cultural changes. One such instance was the move from what I sometimes describe as the "in your face" New Jersey approach to social interaction to the much more reserved Seattle culture where people took turns when merging onto a freeway. As the population and traffic have grown, the Seattle residents of today are less mellow in their driving etiquette. And then there are the climatic changes which have been dramatic for us. Moving from Florida to Minnesota was indeed from one extreme to another. Then we followed it up with moving to the furnace they call the weather in Phoenix. In the course of about six months we went from a low in Minnesota of 45-50 degrees below zero to a high in

Phoenix of 118 degrees, a variance of almost 170 degrees! Our bodies were most confused!

I shoveled a lot of snow in very cold temperatures in Minnesota

Even though moving and working long hours can complicate matters, they do not need to rob you of the pleasures of family life. During the time our daughters were growing up, I rarely missed a swim meet, concert or other significant event in their lives. One can lead a balanced life, but make no mistake, your family's' support and understanding is vital. You cannot have a successful journey without it.

Aside from these challenges for family life, the career manager will tell you that we live in fishbowls. While the elected officials that govern a community are supposed to be the ones in the limelight, make no mistake that many citizens know who the manager is. A small incident made me so aware of this even before I was a manager. While serving as a senior assistant county manager for Hillsborough County, Florida, I was on my way to work one morning. While I lived within a few miles of work, I used the Crosstown expressway for a short stretch. In a few seconds while in my car passing through the toll booth, the operator gives me a quick glance and says, "Assistant County Manager Jim Bourey, right?"

The visibility never really was much of a bother for me. Yes, there was the minor annoyance like trying to get in a workout within a narrow window of time at the local YMCA and people stopping to engage me in an issue they had with the city. However, to me, any such annoyance was outweighed by the reward in playing a major role in helping the community and the appreciation that citizens do have. And it was also during one of those workouts that I learned something special about some city employees. I overheard two people talking about an incident that happened when we were in the midst of a cleanup from a major ice storm. One guy was describing how two employees went to pick up a pile of branches in which his upset young daughter had just lost a significant ring. The two employees painstakingly went through the sticks, branches and leaves and found the ring. The girl was absolutely delighted, and her parents were so impressed with the caring attitude of the employees. He did not know the names of the employees and the staff had not told anyone else. However, soon after, I was at a gathering of all the Public Works employees to thank them for their great work in the massive ice storm cleanup and told the story as an example of terrific service. After the meeting broke up three people came up to me. One had almost dragged the other two and she told to me it was these people that had looked for and found the ring. It was nice to be able to thank them personally. We later recognized these folks at an employee awards event.

For much of my career, I frankly did not know how much people do indeed pay attention and care. I had moved when I left my city or county position. But after working in public service for more than 30 years, I left the Greenville, South Carolina City Manager position and took a private sector position in the city. I was stunned at the number of people who literally stopped as a walked along sidewalks in the downtown to say thanks for my work as the manager. For the first six months, this happened on virtually a daily basis, most of the time coming from people I did not know. And the comments came from all sorts of different people. One day, my wife and I were headed out of town for the weekend and we were stopped momentarily at a stoplight at the edge of town. Someone next to us in a well-worn pickup truck, opened his window and gestured to me to roll my window down. I was wondering what in the world this guy wants, does he want to ask directions, have I absently left my blinker on or did the door close on my coat and it is hanging out? No, he just says, "Thank you, man, for all you did for this city. Bless you." These experiences are not only gratifying but very humbling and help you know you chose the right path.

You can also know you have chosen the right path when you see firsthand the change and improvement in your community. I have to confess that from time to time I have been envious of my wife's profession where she can see progress in her patients, sometimes on a daily basis whereas it often takes a long time for managers to see the benefit of their work.

To those unfamiliar with what a city manager does, I enviably talk about the incredible challenge and reward of managing people. All managers know, they only really accomplish things through others. In some ways, the larger the organization, the truer that is. As the County Administrator for Hennepin County, Minnesota, I had 10,000 employees. But even cities with 15 to 20 employees require the manager to work through staff. To me, a manager's job is principally about how you lead others. This is one of the toughest things in the world but also one of the most rewarding. There is rarely a better feeling as a manager than when you help coach and guide someone to be successful. This will certainly be a recurring theme throughout this book.

In closing this chapter, I need to talk about a manager's stress and stress relief. We have all heard the expression, "It is lonely at the top!" It is not only lonely at times, but it can be quite stressful. A manager must balance the needs of a council, the employees and the public we serve. Later, I write about qualities a manager needs to be effective in doing that, but here I want to just focus on dealing with the stress that it creates. We all handle pressure differently. I am fortunate that as situations become tenser, I tend to relax and not get caught up in the tension of the moment. However, we all need our time away and release from the almost constant pressure. To me, that release became my morning run. Not only did this give me (and still does) time to think, away from the day to day issues but was a balance to the constant sitting in meetings and working at a desk. I have also solved a lot of problems while on that morning run. For a great deal of the time during my career my morning runs would be outside, by myself, no music, just my thoughts to keep me company. With the physical release that running brings, my thoughts come freely and ideas flow easily.

I often feel like a manager sits for a living. That is not good for the human body. However, my running became more than physical activity, time away and stress release, it also became a safe haven from the frustration and disappointment I have experienced in the profession. I have worked for more than 200 elected officials over the years and not all of them have had the community at heart. Not all of them were of sound mind and body. We must always remember; council members are the duly elected representatives of the people and are given the power to make decisions for a community. While I always strived to respect the role of the council and its authority, it is an unfortunate truth that individual council members can be denigrating and nasty. I once sat through a two hour lunch with a council member just chewing on me the entire time with absolutely no substance to her comments. And a council can decide to remove a manager for no other reason than they were not on the council when he or she was selected, and they want to appoint their own person.

So, my running was a release and a counterbalance to the sedentary manager's life, but it was also a coping mechanism for dealing with disappointment. I will talk about how best to leave a manager's job in another chapter. As you leave you need to let go of not only the job but also, the sadness that it may involve. I like to think my running was not a literal running away from disappointment but also part of a renewal process. I am sure it was both.

I admit to some compulsive tendencies in my attention to work and in other aspects of life. Many would think that running up to as much as 120 miles a week or more when I was not also swimming and biking, is compulsive. My wife would call it an obsession. Hard for me to argue it is not compulsive. But human beings are part of the animal kingdom and everyone has a different need to be physically active. However, the more than 150,000 miles I have logged since about 1980 have been as much for the mind as the body. I am fond of doing a "birthday run". When I turned 65, I celebrated with a 65 miles run on my zero runner (a non-impact running machine, you can Google to find out more about it). A nine hour and 15 minute celebration! To find the time to run, I was almost always up by 4:00 a.m., so I could be at work by at least 8:00 or earlier if necessary. In some places, I commuted back and forth from work by running, showering in the basement of City Hall.

I would not recommend or expect anyone to follow my workout routine and I will admit that I can be a bit carried away not only with running but also work. Many of my family and friends would agree with this. However, I hope that everyone that has been a manager has had a stress release valve and those that are getting into a management career find out what works for them to be a counterbalance to your professional responsibilities.

There is a lot of discussion in professional local government manager circles about maintaining a "work-life balance". While city and county management is certainly not unique in those discussions, the all-consuming nature of the job as well as the high level of visibility makes managers particularly susceptible to a work dominated lifestyle. While my professional life required a huge time commitment, I was still able to spend time with my family and be a part of their lives.

I am sure that the size of the communities I served as well as the size of the staffs and budgets did contribute to the demands of my position. The job and family commitments added with my workout routine left virtually no time for other pursuits. My running offered a balance from the work pressures and frustrations but at the end of the day, there was no relaxing and reading a book or doing some other hobby. I have always been an avid reader and early in my career read considerably. As my professional responsibilities progressed, my reading was virtually all professional material, aside from the occasional book I would read while on vacation. I would expect that the work demands of managers in smaller communities would be somewhat less time consuming. My advice is certainly for managers to maintain as much balance in their lives as possible but recognize, the challenges do not leave a lot of extra time beyond work and family commitments.

That is not to say that my wife and I deferred all our adventures. We travelled a good deal, visiting many countries as I said earlier, hiking and camping and eating at excellent restaurants. It helped greatly that Ann would join me on many business trips which even included a weeklong trip to Ireland. Also, while the Newport News City Manager, I led a delegation of people from the business community on an economic focused trip to

China where we visited six cities in ten days and experienced much of the cultural richness of this far away land.

We visited the Cliffs at Moor when in Ireland

This chapter has focused on the motivation, experience and some of the challenges and rewards of being a city or county manager. Each person enters the field for their own personal reasons. Mine were to help make communities better through improving the physical environment, its infrastructure and the socio-economic well-being of the residents.

A street scene in Galway, Ireland

The experience of being a manager was looked at from the personal side of leading a public life and the potential need to relocate, sometimes fairly frequently. The challenge of maintaining a reasonable work/life balance and the need to have a release and counterbalance to the daily work was discussed. While these are indeed challenges, the rewards of helping to improve a community and assisting others in accomplishing their tasks are terrific.

My career journey brought me to many cities where I experienced many different forms of local government and a wide variety of leaders. The next

46

chapter provides a perspective on the variety of forms of local government, including some of the benefits and challenges they present.

There was a surprise snowfall the day we visited the Great Wall

Chapter Two

A Variety of Forms of Local Governance

Local governments throughout the world play vital roles in the lives of their inhabitants. As I have traveled, I have had the opportunity to visit City Halls in many different countries. On the following page, there are pictures from the city halls of Stockholm (above) and Oslo. All of the Nobel Prizes except for the Nobel Peace Prize are announced in the Stockholm City Hall. The Nobel Peace Prize is revealed in the Oslo City Hall.

Certainly, an overwhelming majority of those of us who are or have been professional local government managers believe that the council-manager form of government is the best model for cities and counties to follow. While certainly a strong supporter of this notion, I have also worked in other forms and know the council-manager system is not

without its own set of challenges. This chapter is not intended to be an in-depth exploration, describing all the major local government forms and their benefits but rather to provide some personal observations that may not always appear in discussions about the alternative forms.

Prior to working exclusively for cities and counties with a council-manager form, I worked for four cities with very different structures, including a mayor-council and a city commission. For those unfamiliar with the council-manager form, the council serves in the legislative role and selects a professional city manager (ok, on rare occasions, they sometimes, unfortunately, do not select a professional) who serves as the chief executive of the city. The mayor-council form has two very different variations. In a strong mayor form, the mayor serves as the chief executive. The mayor may or may not be a member of the council which serves as the legislative body. In a weak mayor form, the mayor is part of the council and had no power beyond his role on the council. In a city commission form, the elected mayor and commission serve both as the executive and legislative arms of government. More than one half of the cities in the US and a large number of counties use the city manager form of government. The next most popular is the strong mayor form which is the most common system used in the larger cities in the United States. The weak mayor system is generally used only in smaller cities and towns that do not have as much of a staff. The city commission form is rarely used; however, many counties rely on a version of this with elected commissioners sometimes serving in elected and administrative roles.

Metropolitan Nashville and Davidson County

I started my career working for Metropolitan Nashville and Davidson County (Metro), Tennessee in 1977. While Nashville has a strong mayor, it also has a distinct difference from traditional city governments. Any discussion of governance involving Nashville must include what I consider to be one of the biggest challenges of their system. The 1963 consolidation has had a great many benefits. However, part of the compromise that was made to gain acceptance of the unification was to keep all the districts that existed within the previous councils. This resulted with the creation of, in essence, a mini legislature with 40 council members, only five of which are elected at large. Some county councils in some Midwestern states also have similar sized council or commissions.

In addition to the challenges that a strong mayor form brings, the large council has presented issues for Metro's governance. From my perspective, it has been very difficult for the 35 members elected in districts to focus on the overall community benefit of their actions. It is also difficult for each district member to really understand what is going on in the other districts. A general operating protocol developed, locally referred to as "Councilmatic Courtesy". Unfortunately, this has meant that what an individual council member would like in his district is agreed to by the other members. As you might imagine, this has not always worked so well for things like land use decisions.

While some of the other challenges of the strong mayor form will be mentioned later in this chapter, Nashville suffers to some degree from one of the biggest downsides of a strong mayor, turnover in key positions each time a new mayor takes office. This is not as extreme as in some other locations where, at times, all the department directors may be replaced. Nevertheless, there are some important positions like the finance director that frequently turnover with a new mayor. This practice not only restricts the pool of potential professionals that would be interested in working in these positions and tends to reward political support rather than required skills but it also damages the continuity of governance.

City of Tulsa

After making the decision to leave Nashville for career advancement, I moved on to take a position as a section manager within the Tulsa Metropolitan Area Planning Commission. During my tenure, the section was transferred to the City of Tulsa's Community Development Department. At the time, Tulsa was governed by a City Commission. This form was initiated at the turn of the 20th century in Galveston, Texas, to expedite their recovery from a devastating flood. There are some different variations of this form. In Tulsa, as in other cities, the Mayor and Commissioners were elected to serve both administrative and legislative functions. They sat as the legislative branch to approve ordinances, the budget and make policy decisions but also had administrative roles. This included a Commissioner elected for streets and public property (engineering and public works activity), water and sewer, police and fire and revenue. The Mayor handled administrative matters as well as land use and community development. There were no technical skills required to run for the commissioner positions responsible for various functions. While Tulsa switched from this form, Portland, Oregon still operates with a similar form. The variation in Portland is that the commissioners are not elected as administrators of distinct areas but rather are assigned areas of responsibility by the mayor, who can keep all the areas to himself or herself or delegate to commissioners.

Some of you are probably wondering how in the world this type of governance could work. While it is certainly far from ideal, I was surprised that some things worked rather well in Tulsa. That it functioned with any effectiveness, I attribute to the general quality of the elected officials. With only five elected governing members, the public had a pretty good idea of who they were voting for and could evaluate how they were doing in office. However, I also think that the form was ultimately changed because of some fundamental breakdowns in providing service.

When I arrived in Tulsa in 1979, it was a boomtown. The city had not kept up with the rapidly expanding boundaries and growth. The lack of investment in the water system was a great example. The city kept extending lines further and further out from the center of the city without providing an adequate network of pipes and adequate pressure to serve

52

the development. This continued until outlying customers actually experienced negative water pressure. Instead of water flowing when a resident turned on the faucet, some were greeted by a sucking sound. I am not making this up, I promise. There are other examples of the failure of the system to adequately support the city's development. This included a major breakdown in the drainage system and flood protection which resulted in more than one severe flood.

Cherry Hill Township

From Tulsa I moved on to be the Community Development Director for Cherry Hill, NJ. You will start to see a pattern of increasingly longer moves. Cherry Hill operates under what New Jersey calls the mayor business administrator model, where there is a strong mayor who employs a business administrator to handle the administrative functions and the major department directors report to the mayor. Thus, I reported directly to the mayor. With the functions of my department including planning, land use and community development, there was a lot of interaction with the mayor.

My time in Cherry Hill was most enjoyable as I always had an excellent relationship with the mayor, Maria Barnaby Greenwald, and most amicable relationships with the council members. In addition, while the form of government could produce tensions between the Business Administrator, Ron Miller at the time, and the department directors, I always had a great rapport with Ron. In fact, we became friends and stayed in touch as we moved on. Ron later became the city administrator for Topeka, Kansas, and the city manager for Naperville, Illinois and Aurora, Colorado.

While there was tension at times between the mayor and council, it was less severe than in other locations and the government functioned in a fairly effective way. Frankly, I believe that was the result of the mayor's style which was both what could be call determined yet also open and conciliatory. In addition, Cherry Hill only had about 85,000 people and while we dealt with some significant issues like affordable housing and some major development, it was a relatively settled community without the constant shifting of power between pro-development and anti-development groups, like my experience (and many others) in Florida.

City of Seattle

You know from my previous description, my next move was across the country to be Director of the Office for Planning. Seattle has a strong mayor-council system. However, I would rather liken it to what I would call a strong mayor-strong council system. Seattle has nine council members who are certainly full time and earn more than $120,000 per year. The council selects a President of Council who serves a two-year term. The council has a substantial staff which includes their own staff and a staff for the entire council. This sets up a great competition between the mayor and council which gets in the way of governing the city. The council staff often is in a position of challenging the mayor's proposals. The next step in the political ladder for the full time council members is frequently seen as the mayor's position. This is one of the challenges of the mayor-council form of government, but it is amplified in Seattle where there are highly paid, full time council members. Seattle also does suffer from significant turnover in key positions when a new mayor takes office.

Please know this is my opinion and not necessarily a widely held view but I sometimes feel that Seattle is a dynamic and thriving city not because of the form of government, but despite it. When I left the city in 1987, there were less than 500,000 people within the city's slightly more than 100 square miles. Today the city population exceeds 750,000 inhabitants within the same city limits. No relatively large, already developed city in our country has seen a similar type of growth with no expansion of its territory. Not everyone will agree this great change has been a good thing, but that question must be debated outside the covers of this book.

As with the City of Tulsa, I believe that Seattle has benefited from some fairly enlightened leadership of mayors over the years. These mayors have, at times, overcome some of the challenges presented by its governmental structure. When I worked for the city in the 1980's Charles Royer was the mayor. He was an excellent leader and the city did some progressive things under his leadership. One of the important projects I was involved with during that time was the construction of a tunnel under the downtown. The initial use of this tunnel was to accommodate most of the buses coming to and through the downtown. Thanks to a very robust bus system which carried more than 50% of the downtown workers, the buses were clogging up the street network. The vision was that this tunnel would later be used for light rail when the city built a system. This has indeed happened and it has been a huge asset for that purpose. To build the tunnel in today's dollars would have been enormous.

The city did indeed incur the really large cost of building another tunnel under the downtown in the past few years to relocate the old and earthquake damaged elevated highway, referred to as the viaduct, which for decades cut off the waterfront from the downtown. While this was a very costly project, it has enhanced the downtown immensely. These commitments are most difficult to achieve with the governmental structure as well as the most activist population, with each citizen knowing they have the answer for what is best. It takes a dynamic leader to help make it happen. Mayor Royer served three four year terms, longer than any other Mayor in the City's history. In 1983 Mayor Royer served as the President of the National League of Cities. He moved on to other prestigious positions, including serving as the Director of the Harvard Institute of Politics at the John F. Kennedy School of Government. I was fortunate to get to know the mayor and reconnect with him years later. It will show you how times have changed but some of us knew that Mayor Royer welcomed some staff members to join him on late on a Friday afternoon in his office for a glass of bourbon. We had some interesting conversations during my visits to his office.

Also while I worked in Seattle, the President of the City Council was Norm Rice. He succeeded Royer as mayor. Rice benefited from training he received while obtaining his master's degree in public administration. He not only provided some great leadership for the city but also at the national level while serving as the President of the U.S. Conference of Mayors.

Council-manager system

You probably are thinking that my next move could not be further than the one to Seattle. Well, you are almost correct, but it actually was further. Tampa, Florida is not only a heck of a long way, but it is culturally very different. From my time working as an Assistant and then Senior Assistant County Manager for Hillsborough County, Florida, to leaving my last manager position, I worked in council manager arrangements, with the exception of serving as the Executive Director of the Maricopa Association of Governments (MAG), the regional body for the Phoenix Metropolitan Area. In addition to the positions with Hennepin County and MAG, I served as the Chief Administrative Officer for El Dorado County (more about this job from hell later) and City Manager of Greenville, South Carolina and Newport News, Virginia.

My experience has been that the level of professional management top to bottom in the council-manager organizations I have worked for and observed is superior to those places that do not have a similar governance structure. Appointing a professional manager to lead city or county operations is just generally superior to electing someone who does not have the professional management skill. While managers can come and go, and they certainly do, the staffs are much more stable than in a strong mayor form where the newly elected mayor often feels the need to have their own folks as department directors and even to reward political supporters with positions in the city.

However, nothing is perfect and, I believe, there are some innate challenges that come with a council-manager arrangement as well. The manager serves at the pleasure of the council yet needs to make recommendations for actions which some council members will undoubtedly disagree with and they may end up on the losing side of a vote. Certainly, this can be frustrating for council members that feel they should be able to tell the manager what to do. While the council as a whole appoints the manager and makes decisions as a body, they can be frustrated that as individuals they have no authority to act. I have worked for many council members that do not accept they have no authority as individuals over a manager. As a manager you certainly want to listen to each council member and work to help them succeed with their particular goals. But those things can run counter to the goals of what the full council wants.

A great leader for the Council can be not only great for the manager but also for the community. Hennepin County had a very divided Board of Commissioners, for many years, split along party lines. This made for very difficult relationships among the board members. However, just prior to my arrival as the county administrator, Mark Andrew took over as the chair of the board. Commissioner Andrew truly understood how a great leader could work with people from opposite persuasions and bring about a consensus in decision making. He operated on the premise that the more power you give to others, the more you receive in return. His leadership as the chair helped to make the board operate in a much more collegial fashion, arrive at compromises on issues and move the county forward.

We all know really nice people with great intentions that may have ended up being disappointing in their conduct as elected officials. However, there are also many people who stay true to their values and beliefs and remain steadfast in doing the right thing regardless of the political consequences. The Mayor of the City of Newport News, Dr. McKinley Price, is one such elected official. Currently in his third term as mayor, he has remained a wonderful, giving and caring individual. This is in spite of council members' attacks and having to make tough decisions.

Mayor Price has been a great model for the city. He has always shown exceptional determination and grace under some difficult circumstances. His groundbreaking leadership as an African American dentist in the region paved the way for others. As someone growing up and living in the city except for when he attended college, he experienced the challenges of a racially divided and prejudice society. Yet, he does not let previous unfair and sometimes hostile treatment get in the way of his levelheaded effort to bridge gaps in the community and bring people together. I could not be prouder to call him a good friend!

Additionally, changes in council members can indeed affect the longevity of the manager. Some new council members may just want their person as mentioned before. Some council members just do not understand that a manager can adjust to a different policy direction with the differing views of new members.

There is also an interesting quandary as well in working with the public. Managers want to be sensitive to community concerns and seek community input on projects. However, the manager has to be careful not to get between a council member and his or her constituency. The public role of the manager is covered in a later chapter, but it is certainly a potential pitfall for a manager.

Sorting through all the variations, I must agree with my colleagues that the council-manager form generally provides the best governance model. Albeit, I need to add that so much depends on the quality of the elected officials. I have seen other forms work where there are high quality people in office and city manager run governments struggle. It is ironic and sad that, in my opinion, the City of San Diego changed from a city manager form to a strong mayor not because of the failure of the system but a failure of the elected officials. This statement will be repeated but stated here as well to give emphasis, when a manager examines a community where they are considering employment, examining the city council is critically important.

Strong mayor's Achilles heel

I would be remiss in not offering my opinion on one of the biggest and sometimes hidden differences between a city run by a city manager and a city run by an elected executive who was elected based on politics rather than executive leadership and management skill. It is clear to me that top to bottom there is better professional management with a city manager. I will use an example which is opinion on my part and could be unsettling for some and others in the local situation may disagree. The City of Charleston, SC is governed by a strong mayor. For decades, the mayor was Joe Riley, serving seven four-year terms. By any accounting, Mayor Riley led a renaissance for the city, and it is a most attractive places to move to, as well as visit. He is particularly well known for the redevelopment of the historic area into a vital core that has helped to drive the success for the region. He has won as many awards for his work as any mayor that I can recall.

So here is the catch, while Mayor Riley was amazing at leading the resurgence of the city, there was no professional manager to ensure high quality management in the departments. I believe this helped lead to one of the greatest tragedies in the city's history. In 2007, the Super Sofa Store fire cost the lives of nine city firefighters. What happened is very well documented and has been recounted numerous times by one particular fireman who participated in the event. The loss of life was totally unnecessary and, in fact, it was the firefighters' own actions which helped to create the catastrophe.

Any professional manager who has read the account is surely as sick as I am with the chain of events. One of the firefighters involved in the incident, who so poignantly tells the story, clearly says it was a failure of management. The department had not kept up with professional practices and training that would have prevented the unnecessary deaths. In fact, it was the fire fighters' own actions that drew a fire which had started outside the building into the structure and then caused it to virtually explode with intensity when they broke open windows that fed the fire with the oxygen it needed. The resulting explosive fire then killed nine firemen in the building when the windows were broken.

Would the fire department have been more prepared if the city had been managed by a professional city manager? Would a city manager have ensured that the department used the best current methods and were well trained? We, of course, can never say for sure. In my heart, I know the answer.

This chapter reviewed a variety of types of local government management including the strong mayor, city commission and council manager forms as well as some of the benefits and difficulties with each form. While the strong mayor has a lot of supporters and is especially prevalent in large cities, the competition set up with ambitious council members can be counterproductive, the appointment of politically motivated new department directors and the tendency to not require professional management are all typical drawbacks. City Commission types of government have their difficulties as well and its form is not used that much anymore. However, it was also pointed out that having high quality elected leaders can overcome some of the pitfalls of these forms. While the council-manager form does value quality management, there are certainly challenges with its operation as well. Appropriate council-manager relationships are vital to its success.

We will be exploring city manager roles, responsibilities and actions extensively in this book. So, how does one best prepare to be a city manager? The next chapter provides a perspective on some alternative paths.

Chapter Three

The Path to be a Local Government Manager

In starting another chapter, I feel obligated to say again that the opinions in this book are mine from personal experience and not a set of universally held beliefs by the profession. They are meant to round out what people learn in public administration coursework or at the usual seminars and conferences. This is not in any way to devalue the most important knowledge and perspectives these professional development experiences provide.

The public administration programs in universities across the country have prepared countless city and county managers for outstanding careers. I had the opportunity to teach in a Master of Public Administration program at Arizona State University and have been a guest lecturer on many occasions in a number of university programs. However, there are other paths of education that can also lead to successful local government management careers. I followed one of those less travelled paths with a Bachelor of Environmental Design in Architecture as well as Master of Architecture and Master of Urban Design degrees. The two masters' degrees enabled me to do coursework in many of the outstanding graduate programs at Washington University, including law, business, economics, political science and urban studies as well as architecture and urban design. My goal was to understand our urban areas; their physical make up, economic systems and social fabric as well as how they are governed.

All students of local government management know that the profession has roots in civil engineering. Understanding a city's infrastructure was crucial for the early practitioners. I must express some concern that some public administration programs have moved more and more to focus on public policy and less on operations. Of course, it is all important, but managers must be conversant with the physical city as well as the economic and social fabric. I believe that managers need to have a working knowledge of the water, wastewater, storm drainage and road systems and all that makes up a city.

Beyond the technical side of my education, the design discipline taught me something as valuable: how to approach problems and seek to resolve issues. On many campuses, the architecture students are known for being a lot less traditional than other students. This was certainly the case for the School of Design at North Carolina State University where I did my undergraduate work. You could generally pick us out from the other students in the engineering classes we took with them. The education I received taught me how to see beyond the more obvious solutions to problems which all too often present win/lose outcomes. This taught us how to focus on the type of environment we were trying to create and how to explore alternative approaches. To be able to step back and view a situation outside of preconceived solutions can be vital for a local government manager allowing him or her to find answers for what seem like intractable problems.

While there are different educational tracks professionals take to be city and county managers, there are also many employment paths as well. Some step into a lead management position with a small town, virtually right out of school. This probably involves a lot of baptism by fire! It would certainly be hard for me to be an advocate for this path. There really is a lot that can be learned in local government positions which prepare you for the top job. One could argue there are two fundamentally different paths as a local government employee that could lead to a city/county manager position. Many who hope to be managers start by working in a city manager's office as an assistant to the manager or even assistant manager in some smaller jurisdictions. I have seen many with substantial education that actually even start out as an administrative assistants in order to get a position in the manager's office.

Another common track is to work in a department and gain experience in managing people, projects and programs. This was my avenue to a manager's position. While both paths can work, I would like to comment on the specific value of beginning a career in an operating department. The path I took began in a planning department and then rising to the level of a department director. Working in a department can help one understand how to manage projects and manage people working on projects, in addition to the work of analyzing issues and writing reports, which one will also experience in a manager's office. The direct supervision of employees and projects is an invaluable experience for managers. The understanding of how to develop and execute a schedule and budget for a project is an also an important skill.

In addition to the management skills that can be learned in a department, there is substantive knowledge of city operations that can be gained. Working in a planning department can give one an overall perspective of the city and important issues it may be facing. Similarly, working in a budget office can provide a broad understanding of a city and the entire organization as well as provide important technical financial skills.

While there are many paths that a professional can take to be a manager, demonstrating initiative and taking advantage of opportunities to display your competence is critical. You need to seek out opportunities, not wait to let them find you. I learned this lesson relatively early in my career. When I was working in Tulsa as a section manager in the city development department, the city needed a downtown plan. For historical reasons, the downtown business community did not have confidence in the city staff to do the work. However, over time, I got actively involved in the downtown business community and produced certain pieces of work that were valued, such as helping lead the establishment of a downtown improvement district. I then convinced those I had been working with that I could write the downtown plan. This was not an assignment from my supervisor, and I had to get his approval as well as that of the mayor for me to do the work. I had established a relationship with the mayor by taking advantage of the fact that he came in very early to work each morning. I found that 6:00 to 6:30 AM was a good time to visit with him, with the approval and support of my department director, of course. As an aside, the mayor at the time was Jim Inhofe, who has an interesting political history. He later was defeated by a wide margin in a bid for Congress yet was able to resurrect his career and is currently a US Senator from Oklahoma.

As this chapter has discussed, there are many paths to becoming a city or county manager. In addition to the frequent path through a public administration degree, many other educational avenues are sometimes followed. My architectural background and variety of coursework in different disciplines brought knowledge and an approach to problem solving that has been valuable throughout my career. Whatever path one takes it is important to understand the physical infrastructure that makes up our urban areas.

This chapter also summarized typical paths from an entry level local government position to being a manager, including coming up through a line or staff department or beginning in a city or county manager's office, as well as the how the size of a community makes a difference. It brought out the value of experience as a front line supervisor and project manager.

So there are various ways that people take to become a city manager. Whatever path one follows, I believe there are some important leadership qualities that every manager should aspire to possess. These are described in the next chapter.

Chapter Four

Leadership Qualities

So much has been written about leadership that it is hard to imagine that there could be anything new to say. I do not profess to have innovative approaches to effective leadership that have not already been tried. I do want to present those qualities in a leader that my experience has shown to be the most important. Please do not think I have delusions of always exhibiting these qualities throughout my career. There are certainly too many times to recount of not living up to my own ideal. This chapter describes 14 qualities that I would ask the reader to consider. After reading through this list, you might think that only Superman, or at least a close cousin, could possess all these qualities. They are presented as something to strive for and have served as something for me to aim for, fully recognizing that none of us will achieve perfection. These are not necessarily presented in order of importance as I think they are all important.

Communication ability

It cannot be very surprising that this is the first quality mentioned. There is no shortage of advice in professional literature on good communication. I agree with those that say outstanding communication starts with attentive listening. Sadly, all too often, we are so focused on what we want to say, that we do not hear what others are trying to tell us. Most of you have heard the sage advice, "Seek first to understand and then to be understood." This takes work and discipline and is not something that always comes naturally. One of the most important pieces of coaching I think I provided to my department directors when answering questions from the city council is to be sure to listen to their question and refrain from formulating an answer before the council member finishes asking the question.

One of the tools of communication I really had to work hard on was to let the person I was engaged with know I understood what they were saying. Sometimes, this can involve a lot of head nodding and saying "yes, I understand". Unfortunately, the art of listening is now suffering considerably with the constant attention to our communication devices. Nothing will tell the person you are talking with, "I do not care about what you are saying," faster than checking your messages.

Of course, communication is not all listening; one needs to be able to effectively express his or her ideas in a variety of situations and settings. While speaking to all sizes of groups appears to come more naturally to some than others, training and practice can make a huge difference to those that are less comfortable speakers. Most people are relatively at ease speaking one on one, but even that can be a challenge for the most introverted among us. Being able to clearly and concisely express one's thoughts is so fundamental, that seeking training and coaching is a must for those who need it. And those who struggle with public speaking will never be better at it if they avoid doing it. One technique that was been helpful to me as I sought to become comfortable speaking to groups of all

67

sizes is to envision myself just having an ordinary conversation about things that I would like to talk about. At this point, that idea is so ingrained in me that I do not have to think about it.

Of course, for a local government chief executive, things do get complicated. At this point in my career and life as a public speaker, I can speak with very little notes on any topic that I am familiar with. However, managers know we are often asked to speak at gatherings, on topics that we do not know very well. There is frequently not sufficient time to become as familiar with the subject matter as you would like and, therefore, relying on notes is generally necessary. Learning how to speak from notes and still have some eye contact with the audience is important.

Developing a comfort level in reacting to questions and situations that arise in presentations with audience interaction is also important. Again, listening to the question before developing a response is critical. In situations like this, one needs to be comfortable with taking a bit of time to collect your thoughts and develop a response.

Communication is particularly challenging in a large organization like Hennepin County. While it would be nice if the department directors and middle managers would pass along accurately what the administrator wants to communicate down the line, which is just not what happens. Thus, I felt the need to bring the message, vision, mission and objectives more directly to the entire staff and communicate in person with them. For Hennepin County that included visiting the individual workplaces. I ended up talking directly to about 7,500 staff members to show interest in them and what was happening with their work and the department.

In addition to this, I held a series of meetings to reach out on a regular basis. This included the following:

- A weekly meeting with the assistant administrators and department directors

- A quarterly meeting with all the midlevel managers, approximately 250 people

- A semi-annual meeting with all supervisors, approximately 1,250 people

- A series of brown bag lunches, held in a variety of locations for anyone who wanted to attend

This sounds like a lot but when you are trying to institute change, getting the message out into the organization is critical.

With the City of Newport News, in addition to the weekly assistant managers and department directors' weekly meetings, all employees were invited to attend one of two semi-annual meetings. During each of these meetings which occurred on the same day, one in the morning and one in the afternoon, I gave a brief (five minute) run down of some important issues and then answered employee questions for as long as they asked them. This generally ran from two to two and a half hours per meeting. It was indeed quite a day with all the other meetings fit in between, but the employees responded so very positively to the effort. It was more than worth it.

Enthusiasm and high energy level

We all understand the value of a great pregame or halftime inspirational speech by a football or basketball coach. These are not ho-hum delivered casual talks. They need to inspire the team into action. Managers can and must inspire their teams to act; they must be cheerleaders. In addition, people's actions so often reflect their leader. Style makes a difference. Enthusiasm and high energy are contagious. Being positive is also contagious.

One of the nicest compliments I ever received from an auditor was when I was serving as the County Administrator for Hennepin County.

With an organization of 10,000 employees, you wonder how much people get the message from the manager. The organization was pretty laid back and complacent and things got done in a somewhat uninspired fashion. When I asked the auditor what his sense was of any changes he saw in the organization after I had been the administrator for a while, he said he saw a much greater since of urgency. That was pretty awesome to me. Having a sense of urgency is later in this list.

Facilitation and collaboration

No matter how seasoned you are, everyone knows that studying an issue and developing a recommendation is a small part of being a city manager. It is always more than what one does sitting at a desk and computer. Almost any issue of substance that a manager deals with will have multiple perspectives and well-intentioned people will often have decidedly different views of the matter on the table. A key role that managers so often play is sorting through divergent viewpoints and developing a recommendation that can be good for all or most all concerned. In doing so, it is critical for a manager to have skill in bringing people together, facilitating a dialog and developing approaches that people can embrace. Early on in my career I read the well-known book, Getting to Yes (Roger Fisher and William Ury, Penguin Book, 1983). Its author lays out a great approach to developing agreement by not focusing on opposing positions but rather getting to the heart of what each party would like to achieve; what will really accomplish their objectives. It was written many years ago but it is timeless.

Ability to focus

A manager's job pulls one in many different directions, it often seems, at the same time. Managers move from one situation to another that are entirely different. You can go from a sensitive, difficult personnel meeting to a celebration with employees in a matter of minutes. While you may try to schedule ways to help make a transition, it is inevitable that you will have to shift gears quickly. Managers must be able to focus on the task at hand, be in the present and maintain an appropriate demeanor for the task you are engaged in at the time. Being able to compartmentalize is certainly an advantage. People know when you are truly present and focused on engagement with them. I remember once coming out of an evaluation with the county board which had gone well and heading right into a meeting that involved letting someone go. I was immediately focused on the next task at hand while walking through the County public space. After, someone told me they were worried the evaluation did not go well because I looked so serious. People pay way more attention to the manager than each of us sometimes realize!

Analytic ability

The issues managers face are rarely simple or have obvious answers. Those issues would already have been handled at another level in the organization. While a manager does have staff resources to work through, he or she will often need to employ their analytical skills to address thorny issues. Managers must be able to reason through complex matters and understand the best approaches.

Emotional intelligence

I feel that the local government management profession has danced around emotional intelligence training for so many years without really understanding the incredible importance it has for a manager's success. I have been involved with a great many professional development programs and organizational improvement approaches over the years. It has often felt like the flavor of the month or at least flavor of the year. No other program has been as valuable to me or my organizations as emotional intelligence. People describe emotional intelligence in a variety of ways. To me, it is the ability to have a clear and accurate understanding of how others perceive you, to be able to interrelate to others in a positive, constructive manner and to be in control your actions and reactions in given situations while being true to your own beliefs and not shy away from making contributions as you interact with others. This is so critical that I devote an entire chapter later in this book on the topic.

You will note that although the qualities in this list are distinct and different there is certainly some overlap.

Self-confidence

Managers need to be self-confident. People are reluctant to follow someone that is not sure of themselves. If a manager is not confident, it will be very difficult for the staff to really believe that the direction the manager is leading the organization is correct. Of course, the manager needs to be self-confident without being self-absorbed or arrogant. You cannot come across as a know it all. In fact, it is a good idea that, even when a manager is knowledgeable about an issue, to seek others' perspectives.

Selflessness

Managing is not all about the manager, it is about the community and selflessly serving that community. To me, one of the things that makes me most uncomfortable is the constant use of the word "I" as a manager talks about assignments or a desired path. It should all be about "We". You can replace "I" with "We" in virtually any circumstance. I love it when an MVP in a team sport just talks about what "we" did to achieve the Most Valuable Player Award. It is a recognition that the individual would never have won the award without the team.

Patience with a sense of urgency

Yes, I am serious about having patience but at the same time being able to communicate a need to move forward to accomplish things in a most timely manner. My sport of choice to play and watch is basketball. I apologize to those that may not share the same enthusiasm, but I would like to use a basketball analogy. For those not familiar with basketball, a fast break is when one team gets the ball on the opposing team's side of the court and tries to move with the ball quickly to their end with more players than their opponents and score before the opposing players can get back to defend. When leading a fast break, the person with the ball generally tries to position themselves so that they can either go in for a layup or pass off to a teammate making their way to the basket. In order to beat the other team to the basket, they certainly need to move fast, indeed with a "sense of urgency". However, the person with the ball needs to be patient and smart in their decision making. They want the opposing player who is outnumbered to either commit to guarding them or to guard their teammate before they decide to pass or shoot themselves. They must be patient enough to get the opposition to make a commitment and if they are not, the defender will be able to potentially stop the person with the ball from scoring. This play, which takes a few seconds at the most, demonstrates the need to move quickly but have patience at the same time.

Commitment

I imagine that many of you have heard the story of the chicken talking with the pig about the making of a sausage and egg breakfast. Given the nonchalant attitude the chicken has towards the meal preparation, the pig reminds the chicken that to a chicken the breakfast is but a contribution but to the pig it is a true commitment. You cannot have a halfhearted allegiance to your community and your role, you must be "all in". Councils, staff and residents can sniff out any ambivalence and lack of a full and no holding back effort. While I have worked as a manager in many places, it was always about the place I lived and worked at the time. Communities deserve nothing less.

Flexibility

While we need to be determined to succeed, have confidence in our approach and be committed to stay the course under pressure, managers also need to be flexible and willing to consider alternate paths to a destination. Managers must also know how hard to push and when to back off, at least for some period of time. I had made a recommendation while in Newport News that the council pass a reduction in the taxation rate for private aircraft housed in the city. Newport News was charging owners of planes many times more than nearby cities. As a result, owners were avoiding keeping their planes in the city, despite superior facilities at the Newport News Williamsburg Airport which was in the city. We had studied this and figured out that we could cut our rate by 75%, be more competitive and over a relatively short period there would be enough additional aircraft to actually increase our tax revenues and add to the local economy.

Some council members had a difficult time wrapping their minds around this and the idea was likely not going to fly (apologies to those who hate puns; my family will tell you, I love them). I do have to digress for a moment to tell you about how this played out with one particular council member. I had talked with her one evening and she had told me she was ok with the proposal. However, she called me VERY early the next morning (like 5:30 a.m.) to tell me she could not support it. She told me the night before God came to her and said it was just not right. That, it would only help the rich and not others. She said, "Jim, this is God talking, not me". I was certainly not going to challenge Him on this. Honestly, this is not exaggerated one bit. So, I backed off from moving the idea forward and bought some time to educate the council in a more relaxed atmosphere. The proposal did indeed pass several months later. I guess God came around. The city did get a large influx of planes and more than made up the revenue.

Fortitude

Being a city or county manager is not for the faint of heart. The timid need not apply. There will be times when it takes a great deal of fortitude to work through the rough spots. At times, no matter how hard you might work to obtain a consensus on an issue, it just may not be in the cards. You may face some tough meetings with Council members, employees or the public.

I will not likely forget when some new accounting rules were adopted by the Government Accounting Standards Board (GASB) that changed how local governments accounted for their pension and Other Post Employee Benefits (OPEB). This rule, and a more stringent measure passed after that time, pushed cities and counties to get a better handle on the cost of retiree health care, in particular. As the City Manager for Greenville, South Carolina at the time, I brought to the city council recommendations that would have a relatively minimal impact on retirees but save the City substantial expense in the long run. The city council understood the need for the change and the logic of the recommendation. Then they "generously" delegated the actual decision and implementation to the city manager. The most significant difference for a retiree was to require them to obtain a Medicare supplemental plan with the assistance of a contribution from the city instead of the city providing the insurance directly to the employee. While this was not a huge change for them, explaining that to a room full of 250 suspicious retirees and spouses was challenging. I could have delegated the lead in presenting this to a staff member but there are times when a manager just needs to take one for the team and be as supportive and understanding of the audience's views as possible while absorbing the brunt of unhappy people. Really, it was not that bad, no one threw anything solid and I dodged the barbs tossed my way, and most people ended up understanding the situation.

Good judgement

I feel like some measure of having good judgement may be coached but it also seems like some have it and some appear to struggle mightily. Seasoned managers will tell you that, at times, you have to just shake your head and say, "what were they thinking about?" Most of us surely have many stories that would make each other's hair curl, mine included, despite shaving my head every morning!

Judgement can be affected by lots of considerations that cloud our thinking from time to time. A section in a later chapter is dedicated to a situation where some think my judgment was clouded and I also question whether I did indeed use my best judgement.

Being authentic

Congratulations, you have finally arrived at the last quality, although you can probably think of some that were missed. Just as people can tell if you are not fully committed, they can tell if you are the real deal if you are truly authentic. Staff and council members will look for openness and truthfulness to judge your authenticity. Very few things can undermine your relationships with those that are so critical to your success as a manager than if they feel you are not honest and open with them. In addition, actively sharing things about yourself and, at times showing ways that you are vulnerable will help people know you better and feel you are who you represent yourself to be.

Finding ways to relate to staff can also help to establish authenticity. I have twice participated as a model in fashion shows for the staff as part of an Administrative Professionals Day Luncheon. Each time, luncheon attendees got a kick out of seeing their manager walking the runway. It also helped to show that I did not take myself too seriously. This also demonstrates that you are comfortable in your own skin. Of course, dressing up as a clown for Halloween surely told the staff I did not take myself too seriously.

This chapter has presented fourteen most important qualities for a local government manager. Managers come into the profession with different levels of mastery of these qualities. As managers advance in the profession, they hopefully exhibit more and more of these traits. While we will not all demonstrate each of these qualities, they are presented as an ideal to strive to achieve. All careers involve a learning process and hopefully we all come closer to having leadership traits as we progress in our careers. Whether someone is just starting that journey or transitioning from one position to another, being successful in the job search process is important. The following chapter explores that process.

Chapter Five

The Job Search Process

If there is something that I feel qualified to write about it is probably about getting a job. Since you are reading this and we are not in a conversation, I do not need to listen to a gentle ribbing about my skill at keeping one! I will write later about that and three instances where I did not leave on my own accord. But let's not get ahead of ourselves. In addition to getting positions, I have also served as a search consultant on many local government recruitments.

This chapter will provide pointers that have been most helpful for me including networking, identifying possible positions, applying, interviewing and negotiating an employment agreement. As always, I want to remind the reader that there are loads of references on these topics and I do not profess this to be your one stop shopping guide, you should view this chapter as offering tips to consider. However, my approach has helped me to obtain 12 professional positions in my 43-year career.

Anyone who does not have a position and is seeking one should view the search as a full-time job. The amount of work that is required to do the necessary networking, looking for positions, researching the positions and interviewing is at least 40 hours per week. If you do not have a job, finding one is your job! While knowing how to go about the process and where resources are located is important, there is no substitute for hard work and doing your homework.

Networking

While most job search advisors will tell you that networking is important, it is very time consuming and tedious. So be targeted and systematic in your approach; seek out and meet those that can make a difference in your search. The slogan of using a rifle, not a shotgun, applies here. Before meeting with someone you may not know well, you need to know their background, position they hold, about the company they work for and their interests. You also need to be prepared to articulate your interests. Additionally, you should be ready with a doable ask for them. It must be something they will be comfortable with and can do relatively easily. It could be providing an introduction to someone or providing information that does not compromise them in any way. You need to be very considerate of their time, especially if you do not know them well and show your appreciation for meeting with you. Do not expect immediate returns from these meetings and view it as a process.

In local government management, networking is rarely something that will land a specific position. You are more likely to find and gain traction on positions through formal search processes, so I would advise not to spend most of your time on this pursuit. However, networking should be part of a local government manager's activities even when not looking for a job. It may very well lead to the next position. In addition to Greenville, this also happened when I left my position as City Manager of Newport

News and ended up working for a firm in North Carolina for a CEO I had met while the Greenville City Manager.

In your work life, seek out opportunities to meet others and learn from them. When the Executive Director of the Phoenix regional organization, I helped to establish an informal network of executive directors of Regional Councils in other similar western states' relatively large metro areas. These included Denver, Salt Lake City, Seattle, Tucson and Albuquerque. Each quarter, one of us hosted a meeting in our location and presented what our organization was doing. This was not only a great learning experience but formed some friendships from the experience.

I always say that there is way less than the proverbial six degrees of separation. But then over the years, with the places I have worked and my Outlook contact list of more than 8,000 people, I may view the world from a bit different lens than some others. Those contacts and the people I met during my career led to more than one professional position.

Let's digress for a moment and please think about all those incredible coincidences that have happened in your life. We can surely all tell countless stories of those incredible coincidences, or were they just coincidences? Professionally, I had one of those surprising circumstances. While working in Tulsa, Oklahoma in the early 80s, I met and worked with a professional Chamber of Commerce executive named Rick Weddle. Rick was from the western part of the state, so it was not unusual that he would be working in Tulsa. Fast forward to 1997 when I was serving as the executive director of the regional agency for the Phoenix area. Not too long after my arrival in the Phoenix area, Rick was hired as the Executive Director of the Greater Phoenix Economic Partnership. It was a pleasure to work with him another time. Fast forward once again to 2016 when I was serving as the Newport News City Manager. The Hampton Roads Economic Development Agency (HREDA) was hiring a new executive director and the lead candidate was, of course, Rick. I was not part of the hiring team but did work with him closely for a time after he was appointed as the HREDA President and I served as the HREDA elected chair of the board. Coincidental? Fate? Many people believe in what is referred to as the power of synchronicity, that there is some force pulling some people together. I will not try to convince you but would like a statistician to explain how so many events can occur in people's lives that have an infinitesimally small likelihood of happening. Your professional network can be very valuable.

The public sector search process

How different the search process is today than 43 years ago when I and so many of my friends and peers started our careers. The electronic revolution has put a treasure trove of information literally at our fingertips. My peers will recall going to a library where they had a large selection of newspapers to use for researching articles about cities and their councils. They will remember getting budget documents and comprehensive plans in the mail to study before an interview. While it is so much easier today to get information, there is a greatly heightened expectation of what you should know about a community.

And you must to know about the community before you even apply. You need to tailor your letter and resume to fit the interests and desires of the community. Tweaking your resume to fit the location is a quick process. No longer do you have to totally redo a resume on a typewriter without even a memory. It is time for the younger reader to be laughing hard or incredulous. Granted I was coming out of a design education, but I literally hand lettered my first resume. Of course, coming out of school I could print with great skill. Then, I quickly graduated to press on letters; yes, an entire resume rubbing each letter on one by one. I still have those early versions and look at them when I need a laugh or to see how far we have progressed.

While we are focused on resumes, I will give you a bit of my perspective. It is always mystifying to me why some advocate the idea of putting a job

```
┌─── RESUME ──────────────────────────────────────┐
│                                                              │
│  JAMES  MICHAEL  BOUREY                                       │
│      HOME  ADDRESS      2513  Medway  Drive                   │
│                         Raleigh, N.C., 27608   TEL.: (919) 834-5819 │
│                                                              │
│      BIRTH              Hanover, N.H.,  March  2, 1952        │
│                                                              │
│      MARITAL  STATUS    Single                               │
│                                                              │
│      MILITARY  STATUS   1-H, Civilian                        │
│                                                              │
│  UNDERGRADUATE  EDUCATION                                    │
│      SCHOOL             North  Carolina  State  University    │
│                         at  Raleigh  (1970-1974)             │
│                                                              │
│      DEGREE             Bachelor  of  Environmental           │
│                         Design  in  Architecture  (With  Honors) │
│                                                              │
│  GRADUATE  EDUCATION                                         │
│      SCHOOL             Washington  University               │
│                                                              │
│      GRADUATION  DATE   December,  1976                      │
│                                                              │
│      DEGREES            Master  of  Architecture             │
│                         Master  of  Architecture  and  Urban  Design │
│                                                              │
│      THESIS             Toward  a  Theory  of  Urban  Land  Use │
│                         Allocation                          │
│                                                              │
│  EMPLOYMENT                                                  │
│      Saur/Obrock  Design  Assoc.,  Inc.,  7777  Bonhomme,  Suite  2020, │
│      St.  Louis,  Mo.,  63105,  Fall,  1975,  model  maker   │
│                                                              │
│      Oscar  Mayer  &  Co., Inc.,  3900  Merton  Dr.,  Raleigh, N.C., 27609 │
│      Summer,  1975,  relief  route  salesman                 │
│                                                              │
│      Cast-a-Stone,  1309  Kirkland  Dr.,  Raleigh, N.C.,  Summer, 1973 │
│      Draftsman                                               │
│                                                              │
│  REFERENCES                                                  │
│      Donald  Royse,  AIA,  AIP,  SRT  Architects  and  Planners, │
│      52  Maryland  Plaza,  St.  Louis,  Mo.,  63108          │
│                                                              │
│      Dennis  Judd,  Department  of  Political  Science       │
│      Washington  University,  St.  Louis,  Mo.,  63130       │
│                                                              │
│      Frants  Albert,  AIA,  AIP,  Urban  Research  and  Design  Center │
│      Washington  University,  St.  Louis,  Mo.,  63130       │
│                                                              │
│      John  Powers,  Oscar  Mayer  &  Co., Inc.              │
│      P.O.  Box  2540,  Laurel,  Md.,  20811                  │
│                                                              │
└──────────────────────────────────────────────────┘
```

The resume with press on letters

objective on resumes one submits for a specific position. Worse yet are those that submit a resume with an objective that does not even match the position they are applying for. I have reviewed thousands of resumes and the number of people who do this is astounding. If you are applying for a specific position it seems obvious what you are looking for and this just gets in the way. When reviewing resumes, I want to have the basic information on education and experience up front and not have to search for it. I have always done this and had many search consultants tell me they appreciate the approach. This basic information should not be weighted down with endless detail about the positions. That just gets in the way.

After this basic information you can describe skills and accomplishments. However, I find so much dribble in these sections. I recommend against boasting about skills but rather describe accomplishments. Anyone can claim to have virtually any skill in a resume and to me those claims mean very little. It is the demonstrated accomplishments that count. Avoid the fluff and get to the heart of the matter. I am also turned off by particularly long resumes. I will not read more than two or three pages when going through a lot of resumes. If you have many more pages, you can simply save the effort. Now there are indeed exceptions. I get it if you are applying for an academic position and need to cover your publications.

There is no excuse for not knowing about the community, its issues and the council. It will help you get a position or eliminate you. When interviewing for the Chief Administrative Officer position for El Dorado County, California, I had worked hard on research and committed to memory information about each Commissioner. When asked by a Commissioner about my preparation for the interview, I told them about my research. When a commissioner said, "Ok, Mr. Bourey, tell us what you learned about each of us", I was able to do a few minutes description on each of the five board members, including their backgrounds and interests.

The point is not only to demonstrate an interest in and knowledge of them as individuals and the community but also to send the message that you will do your homework as a manager and work hard for them. When you do the interview which is the next topic, you want to walk into the room with the council, walk over to shake their hands and say, "Nice to meet you Mayor Smith, congratulations on the results of your accomplishments on downtown development."

I know this can be a challenge when you are engaged with multiple searches at the same time. That knowledge comes from personal experience. After deciding to move on from Hennepin County in late 1996, I interviewed with several counties and cities. One week will always stand out in my memory. On Monday, I flew to Los Angeles to interview for the County Chief Administrative Officer position. Since LA County is huge, at the time about 80,000 employees, yet without really a strong manager form of government, I was not sold on the position. On Tuesday, it was off to San Diego County to interview for their County Administrator job on Wednesday. This was indeed more appealing and would have been an excellent position. Thursday, I flew to Virginia to interview for the Chesapeake City Manager position. I definitely took advantage of the flight to reacquaint myself with the Chesapeake City Council.

I managed to go through those interviews with my knowledge of the boards intact, but it was a most interesting week. I ended up finishing second in both Los Angeles and San Diego, having never finished second before. I lost out to a former California county manager in LA. As some of you may know it is hard to break into the California market. In San Diego, they selected a candidate who was a former TRW Vice-President as the commissioners really wanted to go with a private sector person. Of course, that can be a challenging transition and he was gone in less than two years.

While you are doing your research on the council, **please** find out what they are like to work for and what the council dynamic is like. A council that is divisive and nasty to one another and staff is a red flag for the manager as is a high turnover for in the manager position. Seasoned managers all know managers that have gotten stuck in the middle of council's disagreements. Remember, as the council is interviewing you, you need to be sizing them up and determining if you want to work for them. I wish I would have known more about the El Dorado elected officials, more about that sad story later!

As most of you know already, cities and counties will use various devices to narrow down a field of qualified candidates. Often you will be asked to answer a series of essay questions or to do similar tasks. Some of us have been victim to a relatively clueless city that requires all applicants to fill out volumes of material before doing any screening. This benefits no one. Several years ago, I applied for the city manager position for the City of Tempe. I knew the city quite well including some council members, having served as the Regional Council Executive Director a few years before. They had appointed the City Attorney as the interim manager. He swore he had no interest in the position and council said they would not even consider him as a candidate.

There really were no apparent successors from the staff and it was to be an open process. The first mistake they made was to have the human resources staff conduct the process. As part of the application procedure the staff required a regurgitation of every bit of professional information one can imagine to be filled out on a unique online form, most time consuming. They also required each candidate to answer seven essay questions with the initial application submittal. I worked for an entire weekend just on the essay questions. At this point in my career, I was very qualified for the position and went all out. Imagine my disappointment when reading in the newspaper that they had appointed the City Attorney as the City Manager. They conducted no interviews. In fact, no one ever read the applicants' submissions, ouch! Despite this horror story, my message to everyone is to use the supplemental information as an opportunity to distinguish yourself. Yes, it is a lot of work and it may not get you an interview. But if you do not show your best in this process, you will not be successful.

While I would not advise people against participating in a manager search process done by the city's or county's human resources staff, go in with your eyes wide open. I have participated in a number of searches where the staff lead the process but relied on outside professionals for an assessment center or analysis with a good result. However, I also went through a lengthy process competing for the position of county administrator for a large county in California. It came down between me a one other candidate when the personnel director conducted reference checks. It became quite apparent that she wanted the other candidate to be selected. I got reports back from my references that she had been quite belligerent in the conversations and attempted to get them to say something negative. Failing to get what she wanted, she asked for more and more references to call. This will stretch the imagination, but please believe me that she ended up with 27 references for me. I have to assume she got someone to point out something about me she could use, since I did not get the position. This is no knock on the other candidate; he was a qualified professional.

My belief about what happened was only confirmed years later when was having a conversation over dinner with a fellow manager. Upon telling him this story, he had this amazed look on his face and said the very exact thing had happened to him when the same county had conducted the previous search. Same county, same personnel director and same process and result, with multiple requests for references and reports from them of being abused. Oh well, stuff happens!

The interview

So, you have the interview, have completed your homework and the appointed day arrives. I am going to assume you have worn your best suit and tie, not a sport coat and khakis, and similar spiffy attire for the ladies.

That is, unless you have been specifically directed to be casual. When you walk in the room, regardless of the shape of the room or where the Council members are, go and shake their hand, making eye contact and referring to them by name. Physical contact is important, as is smiling and being friendly. Thank them for the opportunity to interview.

Interviews will take place in all types of circumstances. Some may actually be televised live and some may have a large, in person, audience. Logistics can be a challenge. I once interviewed for a county administrator position with Kalamazoo County, Michigan in a council chambers with the council at the dais and the audience to my back. After I greeted the council, I turned and addressed the audience and apologized that my back would be to them, but I still considered them very important and valuable to the process. After that, I turned my FULL attention to the council. When interviewing for the county administrator position for Alachua County, Florida, my wife got a chance to see my performance live on their video streaming service. At least someone would be a supporter! I did get a job offer from Alachua County.

One needs to be prepared for about anything. While interviewing for the Chief Administrative Officer for Los Angeles County, I was in quite dark room with bright lights shining on me with the commissioners some distance away and barely visible.

Regardless of the setting, one needs to be relaxed and show that award winning smile. Yes, the interview is about answering questions in a professional and impressive fashion, but it is also very much about making contact with the council. They will hire someone who is an accomplished professional who they believe can perform well in the position, but they will not hire someone they are not personally comfortable with, period. Remember that while the council is generally interviewing a number of candidates, it is really about the fit for the organization. Reminding yourself of that will help you be more relaxed and focus on demonstrating who you are and your best qualities. Show your human side through a bit of humor if the opportunity presents itself. When I was interviewing with the city council for the Newport News City Manager position the city clerk and human resources director were outside of the room and later remarked to me about all the laughter coming from the room.

In an interview with a full council, generally each member will be asking questions. While you obviously are answering the question of a particular council member, do not turn your attention exclusively to that individual but rather continue to make some eye contact with all the members and keep them engaged with your answers. You want the attention of all members throughout the interview. In answering questions do not hurry through your responses, it is not a race to see who can finish first. Rather, be thoughtful and take your time.

Always come with some questions of your own. I generally try to focus on what the council is looking for in a new manager and what their top priorities are. I have also asked if there is anything else that they would like to know about me. In addition, come prepared to give them some suggestions to handle issues they are facing. I always preface my suggestions with a statement to the effect that while I have studied the community and the issues, there are additional things I would learn when the manager, but on my initial review, I would suggest you consider …

Very often you will be asked to give your vision for the organization or community. The interviews for the Greenville City manager position lasted over two days. The first day was individual interviews with each of the council members and the second with the full council. The evening after the first day, I drafted a vision statement for the city based on my conversations with each of the members and presented it to the full council. They appreciated the vision and effort. I hope most everyone knows never to ask them about salary or benefits.

While you should not ask about salary, during the interview or in the course of the recruitment you may be asked what you would want for a salary. I avoid answering with a direct number like the plague. This is a no win for the candidate. If the number you suggest is too low, you have a new built in ceiling for the offer you will receive if you get an offer. If the number is too high, you may scare them away from making an offer. One should always find out what the previous manager made and what the managers in nearby similar positions are making. Those salaries are generally not hard to find.

My response to a council's salary question is along the lines that a salary offer is really up to the council; I have researched what the last manager (or current) made as well as other managers in the area and do not believe we will have any problem coming to an agreement over an appropriate compensation package. Since the council generally has had my salary history, I might reference that as well. If the position would be a clear advancement that I would hope the council would recognize this is a step up for me and they would take that into consideration when making an offer. I have been asked the salary question many times, never given them a number and the council has never pressed further. If the council really pushes you on that, it is at the least a bit of a red flag. In one situation where I was the favored candidate, they went with a second choice because they knew they could get him to agree to a salary that was under the market rate. That was totally fine with me, as it would not have been good to work in a position where that was the value system of the elected officials.

At all times when going through a recruitment, be upfront and open with the recruiter and city/county people you come in contact with during the process. If you are asked for your salary history or what you are currently making, lay it out plainly and simply. People tend to play games and round up significantly. It is amazing how some forget the rules of rounding up and $119,100 becomes about $120,000. Just as any resume inflation is unethical and flat out wrong, so is fuzzing up a salary.

Transparency and ethics

I strongly urge one to be open about their job search. If this is the only position you have applied for, tell them. If you have other possibilities in the works, tell them that as well. If you are going through the interview process with more than one place at a time, you need to be very open and rigorous in how you handle it. This becomes very important if you are offered a position and are still in an interview process for another position. If the position you have been offered is truly the one you want, great, accept the offer. However, make sure you are ok with the terms of the offer. Remember, the ICMA Code of Ethics says that if you accept a position, you are committed to taking that position.

On the other hand, if the position you have been offered is not the preferred position of those you are interviewing for, you have a decision to make. Do you accept that bird in the hand or keep trying to grab the second one from the bush? I will describe two different circumstances which were very challenging for me to illustrate this.

I have been fortunate to have received multiple job offers simultaneously three times. The first was relatively straight forward. Back in 1979, I interviewed at the American Planning Association Conference for several positions. This was a sanctioned part of the conference. I was shocked to receive four offers of positions with Tulsa, Fort Worth, Oklahoma City and Annapolis. Since the Tulsa position was the best for me at the time, the answer was pretty straight forward.

However, in 2003 the situation was not so simple. I was under consideration for the chief executive officer for both El Dorado County and San Bernardino County, California. I kept both search firms informed about the process in each of the searches. The interview for El Dorado County was scheduled well prior to the interviews for San Bernardino County. After the interview with El Dorado County, I was selected as their desired candidate. I decided that I was willing to take the El Dorado County position **if** they made a reasonable offer. I told the search firm I would take the position under the condition that it was an acceptable offer. I told the search consultant for San Bernardino County that I had been selected and would take the El Dorado offer if we could agree on the terms.

In response to this news, the San Bernardino Council accelerated my interview with them, so that they could make me another offer. I informed the search firm for El Dorado County about the San Bernardino interview. Since I did not yet have an offer from El Dorado County, I did participate in the interview. After the interview, El Dorado County made an acceptable offer to me and I accepted the position. In hindsight, the decision to take the El Dorado position led to a lot of disappointment. Once again, more about that later.

In 2013, I was faced with an even more challenging situation. I was in three search processes and ended up with three offers. Over the course of many weeks, I had been in a conversation with the President of the University of South Carolina Upstate to be a Vice-Chancellor and lead their Greenville Campus. They had a rather extenuated process that had to be followed and the President was attempting to get a salary that would make sense for me. During this time, I interviewed for and was offered the position as the County Administrator for Alachua County, Florida. However, the commission ended up playing a public game over the salary they would offer me. As I mentioned earlier, this was a very public process. In a televised commission meeting, they discussed the compensation package they were going to offer me. I was not at all sure that we would reach a competitive salary. I made no representation about whether I would take the position. However, I did need to make a counteroffer to the low initial proposal or walk away from the position. I decided to make a counteroffer I was comfortable with and one that I would have accepted.

After the interview with Alachua County, I was offered an interview for the position of City Manager for Newport News, Virginia. At all times through this process, I kept all the parties informed of my situation with each of these positions. In fact, the City of Newport News could watch the situation with Alachua County playing out live on television. The process in Newport News was set up to be a series of two rounds of interviews. The council was going to narrow down the initial group to two or three candidates for the next interviews. However, after the first interview the council was unanimous that they wanted to hire me. At this point, I decided and informed all parties I would take the Newport New position if we could agree on a contract.

Alachua County had not accepted the offer that would have been ok with me and had not made a counteroffer. I withdrew from consideration since even though I had not committed to Newport News, I believed we would reach an agreement and it was my preferred position. I also told the President of USC Upstate, I was going to accept an offer from the City of Newport News. All worked out fine from my perspective, but it was a very nerve-racking time and I worked very hard to be open with all parties and keep them informed all the way along. If Alachua County would have made a reasonable offer, I would have gone to work for them. This all played out in the Gainesville press and they were critical of the county commission for not making a market rate offer.

Contract negotiation

There are lots of great references for instruction in contract negotiations. Quite a number of years ago, I served on an ICMA Task Force charged with writing a model employment agreement and authored much of an earlier version. The current ICMA Model Contract does an excellent job of going through all the issues to consider and provisions that should be included in a contract. While this is a very complete and great resource, the format is less usable as a go by in creating an actual agreement and I end up relying on some of my past contracts in creating a draft when serving as a search consultant. With all the reference material available, my comments here will be focused on some important provisions in the contract and negotiations on the contract.

Many managers employ an attorney when negotiating an employment agreement. Although using an attorney for advice once when negotiating a separation agreement, I have not used one for an initial contract. I felt that with my experience and the resources at my disposal, an attorney was not necessary. I also did not like the message that it could potentially send to the city council; why did I feel the need to have an attorney to negotiate with my future bosses on my behalf. Did I not trust them?

In negotiating a compensation package and other benefits, I have always taken the view of not pushing the council to the limit. I have been willing to even leave something on the table. I have not wanted to pollute the water and hurt the relationship with the council. To me it was not worth the few extra dollars that could be gained. As in the case with Newport News, I just accepted the compensation offer they gave me. I did push for some non-salary items like the vacation accrual rate and the amount of accrual allowed. I also was provided with an upfront allocation of vacation time.

Always remember the compensation package is more than the base salary. Most seasoned managers recognize that it is easier for the council to provide some compensation in the form of deferred compensation than having it all in base salary. Providing other benefits, such as a car allowance is also another way to boost compensation. So, when you do your research on the market on compensation, be sure to learn what other managers receive in total compensation. And wherever you can, be sure to have non-salary compensation included in retirement calculations.

Some may disagree with me, but I would never take a manager position without some form of reasonable severance. I have had anywhere from six months to a year, except in one situation that will be explained shortly. With the current intense public scrutiny, it appears more and more difficult to get up to a year of severance, but six months is a must. If you look at the time it takes to go through a public search process, it is tough to get another position any quicker than six months and it can certainly take a lot longer.

The one exception to achieving at least a six month's severance was when taking the position of County Administrator for Hennepin County. Because Hennepin County is so large and so visible, making up a quarter of the state's population and the County Commissioners are so influential, the somewhat envious State Legislature has passed certain statutes applying just to the county. In many states it is not legal to pass laws only applying to one place. One of the laws is that the county administrator can only be granted two weeks of severance. So, there was a need to be creative. I proposed to the commission and they agreed to provide me with a beginning vacation balance of six months and allow an unlimited amount of accrual and further that I was entitled to cash out any vacation time at my departure. Not only did this give me severance, it also gave me the payout whether being forced out or leaving of my own free accord. Of course, this deal was even better than a traditional severance.

It is a very involved story and I will spare you all the details, but this arrangement was challenged by the sitting state auditor because of a Minnesota state law restricting the salaries of all government officials to 95% of the Governor's salary. The contract provision was judged to be legal and appropriate by the state attorney general. I have always tried to get an unlimited accrual of vacation as it is hard for a manager to take all the time that is earned.

Most manager employment agreements provide for a periodic evaluation of the manager. While this is certainly a reasonable provision and can be helpful, it can also be unproductive. From my experience, the challenge is that most council members are not very prepared to conduct an evaluation. While councils frequently rate my performance as excellent, there have been individual council members pick at a single thing that did not go the way they wanted. While it is the full council that makes decisions, individual council members still want their way. And then

94

there is the euphemistic "management style" comments. My experience is that this generally is a subterfuge for a staff member complaining to a council member who they know well about something the manager did that they did not like.

My advice is that if the council wants an evaluation and, indeed, this is something that is in the ICMA Model agreement, that there be some process set out in the agreement. Involving an outside professional in the process can be beneficial if the council is truly interested in an objective evaluation.

Along with an annual evaluation, employment agreements will generally also have a clause providing for potential annual salary increases. Some agreements will call for the manager to receive any across the board increases that the other employees are provided. This makes it easy for the council to quietly raise the manager's salary. I have never pushed for that because managers are just not like other employees for compensation. It also sets up a perceived potential conflict of interest for any recommendation the manager might make for an employee increase. In addition, in the current climate of public employee salaries, I am a strong advocate of pay for performance and merit-based pay.

Just as an agreement needs to contain a severance provision, there also needs to be a provision paying for relocation. After paying for my relocation from New Jersey to Washington State to take a department director position, I promised myself it would be the last time. Seattle viewed the city as so desirable that either local people would be available for any position or people would be willing to pay to relocate. Many people in the city appeared to be underemployed because they did not want to move out of the area to get a promotion. It was very difficult when I decided to take that step and relocate in order to advance. It took us over 30 years to get back to the Seattle area where my wife and I intend to spend the rest of our lives.

The most important part of relocation is obviously moving the household, but temporary living expenses and some travel back and forth if your family is not able to come with you is very important and can take some of the sting out of a move. I am not as bullish about other things such as paying for realtor's fees or the sale of a home as it gets to be a bit dicey in the public's perception. Although it can also be a public perception challenge, I have asked for and had included a provision for the city or county to pay for the taxes due for the relocation benefit. If you do not have this provision, generally referred to as "grossing up" you will be getting benefit from only a percentage of the actual relocation paid to you.

One last significant issue on employment agreements is the term of the agreement. Most people like to think in terms of a set number of years for a contract. This presents some practical challenges and I have always negotiated an evergreen agreement, one with no expiration date. I have successfully argued that my employment could be terminated at any time by the Council, so putting a limit on the agreement was really irrelevant.

Contract expiration dates present the council with an affirmative decision they need to make to renew the contract. If one or two councilmembers have a bee in their bonnet at the time of that vote, there can be unnecessary rancor. Another issue is dealing with severance; one would need a provision that if the contract is not renewed the severance would be paid. This provision could be somewhat hard for some council member to agree with. So, people look to complicated schemes that the council must tell the manager some time frame (usually equal to the time of the severance) before the contract is set to expire whether it will be renewed. Again, an unnecessary vote. There are all sorts of machinations I have seen, virtually all requiring an affirmative vote to keep the manager employed.

Negotiating a contract can be fairly tricky if there is no history of the location having good contracts for previous managers and if there is no professional search consultant involved. I always relied on the search firm, where there was one, to help the council understand the reasons behind the agreement and certain provisions. I also like to use the ICMA Model as a base which I could represent as a generally accepted standard.

This chapter has suggested approaches to assist obtaining a local government manager's position, including the following:

- The critical importance of doing your homework to learn about opportunities, the councils, the issues and prepare for the interview

- Coaching tips for the interview including making personal contact and remembering that you are interviewing the council at the same time they are interviewing you

- How to ethically handle interviewing in multiple locations and working with multiple job offers including being open with all parties and only accepting an offer when you are committed to that position

- Important considerations in negotiating an employment agreement including two critical takeaways for contracts: to remember the opportunities that non-base salary compensation such as deferred comp and vacation leave can have

So when you start that new manager position, what can you expect to be some of your challenges? While it may not be an actual minefield, as you will see in what follows, there are certainly many pitfalls to watch out for!

Chapter Six

Navigating the Minefield

Chapter three explored some of the issues with the council manager form of government. This chapter will delve into more detail about some of the challenges facing a manager through describing many of my experiences. Please note these are minefields and the stories are not always positive but hopefully there are things that can be avoided.

Individual council member vs. the whole

One of the most significant issues that managers face is that individual council members would like to see their personal wishes fulfilled. However, the council is the decision-making authority, not an individual council member. An individual council member has no actual authority by themselves. To the newly elected council member this often comes as a shock. In order to get what they want, a council member will often put pressure on a manager to either directly take the action they want or make a certain recommendation to council. That may or may not be something that would be the best recommendation to make. And if the manager were to make the recommendation, it may or may not be what a majority of the council might want to do.

While serving as a manager, I was placed in a most difficult situation by a board member who clearly wanted to manipulate the process to get what he wanted approved as part of a union contract negotiation. While there were more than ten unions, the lead union, the American Federation of State, County and Municipal Employees (AFSCME) had by far the most employees in the organization and the contract provisions that were negotiated with them would generally end up in the other contracts as well. It was the manager's responsibility to negotiate the contract provisions and bring it to the council for approval. The council was not allowed to change any provisions but could only approve or reject the proposed contract. If the contract would be rejected, it would have to be renegotiated. While the Manager could include provisions that were personally favored, he or she ought to negotiate items that would be in line with the policy directions of a majority of the council.

While in negotiation, one council member called me to his office to tell me to include domestic partner benefits, such as access to health insurance, in the contracts. This was in the 1990's when domestic partner benefits were not generally provided. While personally being very favorable to including those benefits, I did not believe that a majority of the council would want to see them as part of the contract. However, the council member knew that if they were included in the recommended contract, it would have been difficult for the council to reject the entire contract and incur the great displeasure of the unions.

So, should I risk the ire of this council member or the ire of the council members that would be opposed to the provision? My belief was that whether to include these benefits should have been a call of the majority of the council. So, I took advantage of a provision in the state law that allowed me to go into an executive session of the council and ask them their preference. Any direction they gave would be held confidential until the approval of the contract.

The decision of the council was, as expected, against including the benefits. While this was the most appropriate way to handle the situation and a majority of the council was pleased with the outcome, it did not endear me to the council member who wanted them included.

Unfortunately, while majority rules, one or two council members can have a great influence on a council which may not even agree with his or her position. I have been in more than one situation where one or two council members that are unhappy with the manager can push the full council to take action against the manager. Council members have said that they support me but are tired of hearing the dissenting council member complain and are giving in to them to bring peace to the council. Sometimes the price of peace can be the departure of the manager.

I never like to introduce a problem without suggesting some solution. However, the best I can do is to raise awareness of this challenge and urge managers to always work to continue to strengthen relationships with all council members and focus on issues that are important to each of them and that a majority of the council will support.

You cannot please everyone, just do what is right

Just as you cannot always please every council member, you cannot always make recommendations which will be universally supported by the public. This is especially true when the citizens do not act in their own best interest. As the Newport News City Manager, I dealt with an issue that had been kicked down the road for many years. It was the operation of what was referred to as the City Farm. This was a minimum security jail facility located on a piece of prime real estate, on the western boundary of the city along the James River. The facility once was an actual farm operated largely with labor supplied by the inmates of the onsite jail.

Over the years, the farming activities had largely ceased. A few cows still occupied the farm but the inmate work responsibilities were principally public works support tasks which included landscape and other maintenance activity. Additionally, the census of the once overcrowded central jail had been reduced substantially through the construction of a regional jail which was built and operated under a partnership of Newport News and three other cities. The function City Farm served, to accommodate an overflow of inmates, was not as necessary as it had been, so there was less need for this extra lockdown facility. For many years, the buildings had been allowed to deteriorate and were in need of significant capital investment to bring them up to more modern day standards. The facility also presented a substantial security risk with a number of inmate escapes.

For those not familiar with Virginia local government law, cities are not actually part of counties. As a result, services normally provided by counties, such as the court system, are provided by cities. Newport News not only has a police department but also an elected sheriff who is responsible for, among other things, operation of the jail. However, the City Farm was operated by a separate department under the direction of the city manager.

In order to develop a good understanding of the existing City Farm jail facility and its operation, we hired a consultant to evaluate the existing jail facility. This study showed the need for a capital investment of more than $10 million. In addition, the study showed that there was sufficient capacity to house all the inmates in the central jail facility. We developed a recommendation that would not only eliminate the need for the ten million dollar capital investment but also save $2.5 million in annual operating cost. This included shifting the inmates to the central jail and eliminating the City Farm department. The Sherriff agreed to take on housing of the additional inmates with no increase to his current budget. In addition, the inmates would still provide the cost efficient public work services they had been providing. Sounds like a classic win/win scenario. Well, not exactly. Neighbors in the surrounding area were not thrilled with the jail operation being eliminated.

I know that may sound a bit strange. As the property had been developed in the area of the City Farm, the new residents were generally comfortable with the housing of inmates nearby. Additionally, a relatively large park had been developed from some of the excess land of City Farm. What the residents feared is that the land would be developed for more residential use. Since this land was adjacent to the very wide James River, over four miles across in some places, it was indeed a great piece of real estate, about 50 acres of which could developed for high quality residential use. Many residents thought the city would close the City Farm operation in order to sell the property to a developer. In fact, some possible development scenarios had been put together in the past.

In general, if you were to ask a neighborhood if they would prefer a jail facility or high end residential developed on property next to them, I seriously doubt you would hear a jail as their preference. Nevertheless, many neighbors organized to oppose the closing of the jail and I became an unpopular figure in the community with my recommendation to do just that. This was despite the fact that I was not entertaining any plans at that time to develop the property. The city council held a number of meetings to discuss the closing and listened to many resident objections and did vote 6-1 to close the facility. We saved $12.5 million in the first year and recognized a $2.5 million annual benefit. While it was totally clear that this was the best path forward, not everyone saw it that way.

Lack of civility

While working with city councils and the public has never been for the faint of heart, the growing lack of civility of the public and city councils themselves, sometimes makes me believe that city and county managers should get combat pay. It is pretty clear that the lack of trust in government has increased significantly over the past decade. This is evidenced in the amazingly low approval rating for the US Congress. This lack of confidence is not reflected in surveys of the public's views of local government services. I have seen this repeatedly in the ratings citizens provide on the services in the cities where I have managed. For instance, I was particularly pleased that in one survey we conducted, 100% of the respondents rated the fire department services as excellent. I have seen this in many other cities as well.

Despite the fact that citizens may have a good reaction to the local services they receive, I believe the frustration they feel with the lack of responsiveness at the federal and sometimes state level, manifests itself at the local level. That is because of the ease of going to meetings and expressing your opinion. Virtually all local governments provide some opportunity for citizen comment at public meetings. This is certainly the right and appropriate thing to do and must continue. This outlet does give a chance for citizens to vent their frustrations with government even if it is not related to what is going on in the city.

This situation is exacerbated by a lack of trust that government officials are telling the truth. Again, while this is driven more from levels beyond local government, the forum for their expression is readily available at council meetings. I need to hasten to add, that many citizens do disagree with local decisions and come to express their frustration on those decisions. My point is the extreme lack of trust and, even dislike, has gained great impetus from the frustrations beyond the local government.

This incivility is not reserved for just citizens. Many managers can relate stories of aggressive and downright nasty behavior of council members to one another. I have heard stories of food fights and literally, punches thrown. While not directly involved in one particular situation described to me by a council member, I have heard this same event confirmed by others. In this council in a location where I worked after this incident, the board members were constantly at odds with one another. While the members were not elected through a partisan political process, it was still dominated by Democrat vs. Republican politics. The two leaders on each side had been especially at odds with one another. One day the leader on one side, we will call him Jeff (not his real name) called up the leader on the other side, we will call Steve (not his real name either), and said it was time to put their differences aside for the best of the community. Steve was pleased to hear this. Jeff suggested that they meet at a particular bar and have a drink to discuss how they could better work together. Steve readily agreed. When Steve arrived Jeff was waiting at the bar for him. After their greeting, Jeff proceeded to serve Steve with papers for a lawsuit he was filing against him. So much for working together in the interest of the community.

Of course, when there are strong differences in the board, a manager can get caught in the middle between the sides pressuring him or her to do what they want. I know managers will agree with me that this is a most uncomfortable place to be!

Win the war not necessarily the battle

There have been times when I had to ask myself, how important is it that the council or commission goes along with my recommendation, especially if there is a significant cost to gaining that approval. While serving as the Senior Assistant County Administrator for Hillsborough County, I was faced with this dilemma. When I was presenting a land use plan to the county commission, one of the commissioners disagreed with a provision in the plan. I had an excellent relationship with this commissioner as she had been a department director before retiring and being elected a commissioner.

When this commissioner raised her objection, she gave me a look that basically said don't you dare challenge me on this, that it was important to her. While feeling quite confident that I could convince a majority of the commission to support me on the issue, it was not that important to the plan and I did not want to push it against the will of the commissioner. If it would have been really important, I would have pushed the board to support the provision. Since it was not, I did not press it. There are times when discretion is indeed the better part of valor.

As mentioned earlier, there is also a time to push a recommendation and a time to back off and pursue it later. Here is another example of this. While the city manager for Greenville, I was involved in an effort to renovate a large relatively dated convention center that the city had purchased from a private entity. We were able to get federal and state funding to assist with the renovation. I proposed that the council agree with obtaining naming rights from a company to add to the money for renovation. Since this was not a common practice for such facilities at the time, the council very reluctant to support the idea. It was obvious the council was not going to agree with the concept at the time since it was new to them and they did not fully understand how it would work. We took a step back and worked to educate the individual council members and demonstrate the value that the naming rights would bring. Later, when we brought this up, the council supported it and the revenue from naming rights played a key role in filling out the revenue needed for a $30 million dollar renovation. This resulted in a modernized facility that has served the community for a long time.

Visibility of the manager

The widely accepted norm in the local government management profession is that the elected mayor and council are the highly visible and out-front leaders for a city or county. I totally buy into this concept and have always honored the important public role they play. So it goes, the manager is the behind the scenes person to carry out the policies of the council. However, I think that most managers agree that the manager cannot effectively carry out his or her responsibility in total anonymity. There needs to be some form of public role for the manager. In addition, the public is interested in knowing the person that has a great deal of influence on the delivery of key public services. There is also value in the public having a measure of confidence in not only the elected officials but in the manager as well.

The question then becomes, how visible should the manager be and how can a manager ensure that their visibility does not outshine the elected officials? This becomes more complex when the council says to a manager, as they did to me when I assumed the City of Greenville Manager position, that they wanted me to be very engaged with the community and very visible. Although this was not the case in Greenville, it is even more complicated when you have a mayor that shies away from the spotlight and pushing the city's agenda.

As the Greenville City Manager, I followed the direction of the mayor and council and was very engaged with the community. Given my critical role in carrying out major city initiatives, some of which will be detailed in later chapters, I became the go to person for the media. While trying to deflect this as I could, to the mayor and council, they were not generally available and did not step up to bring the city message to the public. Also being very active in the philanthropic community, especially the United Way, brought me into further contact with community leaders. A later section in this chapter is subtitled, "Be careful what you ask for, you may get it!" The Council did not really fully understand what it was asking me to do and the fact that almost the entire council turned over while I was the manager led to my notoriety being resented by a couple of newly elected council members.

So, should I have resisted being shoved into the spotlight? Should I have pushed the media away? These are legitimate questions. But it is also legitimate to ask if I would have been as effective in getting things done had I not been as visible a presence and as much of a civic booster? These questions must be taken together. It is hard to believe that we would have been as successful had I been solely behind the scenes. I think it is highly

106

probable I would have served as the city manager for a longer time, if I had been less visible. Maybe it is the Satchel Page, "Don't look back" in me or maybe it is my proclivity to push the envelope, but I am comfortable with how I played it. My philosophy is that I would rather spend a bit less time with a community and get more done than to see things slowly evolve. Sometimes, timing for development is critical and if you sit back and let an opportunity go by, you will not get one again for some time. This is one of those points where some of my manager colleagues may have a bit of a different perspective, and I understand that.

Being a change agent

Some managers gravitate to cities or counties that need a lot if fixing. Whether by a natural tendency to tackle demanding jobs or just the luck of the draw (or lack of it), I have ended up in professional situations that required substantial improvement and/or the council wanted to see a great deal of change. It is exciting and rewarding to guide an organization through a great deal of change and improvement. It is also as challenging and difficult as it is rewarding.

However, all jobs that are going to require the manager to be a change agent should come with a *caveat emptor* label warning, buyer beware. Generally, people are not too fond of change. They find it disruptive and unsettling, not to mention that when there is change, there are generally perceived winners and losers. The manager will likely gain supporters for a job well done but will also get detractors regardless of how well the process went and the benefits achieved.

While the council may be big cheerleaders of the manager as they go through the change process, they also often listen to the detractors and hold actions taken against the manager. Councils most often do not have a realistic view of the change process and think it can happen without ruffling any feathers. Any manager that believes that is possible is in for a rude awakening. And the bigger the change that is needed, the greater the chance of unhappy employees undermining the manager.

With the disruption that change brings which can rub off on the council, the road to a stable, long tenure of the manager is made difficult. Most managers that must bring about a significant amount of change end up having much shorter tenures than those that do not have to follow that path.

This appears to be exacerbated when following a long tenured manager. While it is not something for which I have statistical evidence, I believe that over the course of a long tenure, a manager builds up a great deal of influence beyond their real authority. Council members, many of whom may not have been around for anywhere near as long as the manager and are much less knowledgeable, are often more deferential toward the manager than they would someone with a shorter tenure. New council members are much more willing to challenge a manager if he or she has not built up a level of community support and influence.

However, that does not mean the deferential council members like deferring to a long-time manager. At the time that new manager comes in, they often will flex their political muscles, leading to a more tenuous position for the manager. When the council has not felt they have been able to influence the direction of the city or county as they would have liked to, they often want significant change. At the same time, they are not necessarily willing to ignore employee complaints about the change. All this leads to a much less stable situation for the manager, thus *caveat emptor!*

One would think that I am pushing managers not to be change agents. Not at all. Many communities need change and managers can make an important difference leading that change process.

Council-staff communication

In a theoretical, perfect world there would be a free flow of information between staff and the council, while the role of the manager is respected. And further, all direction by the council goes through the manager and they are informed by the staff on any important issues the council brings up in conversations with them. Experienced managers know that is far from what happens in reality. This is especially true when council members believe they would be more effective in getting the staff to do something if they bypass the manager or, on the other hand, when the staff is in a disagreement with the manager on an issue or the way he or she is leading the organization. This situation can be precipitated in a time of change and there is dissent among some staff that may be negatively affected or disagree with the change.

This can become a slippery slope very quickly. Any attempt by the manager to limit communication between the council and staff is generally met by a great deal of pushback from the council. They will accuse the manager of micro-managing the staff and muzzling employees. At the same time, allowing a continued undermining of the manager is also problematic. The answer, it seems, is fairly straightforward; that the manager's message should be that staff is allowed to talk with council members, but they cannot go to council to advocate for positions against a manager's decisions. Also, a council member cannot give direction to staff to do things that the council member would like to see done. I have tried hard to get that clear message across but when you have some that would intentionally misrepresent a manager's policy, it becomes a challenge. Being clear on the issue of appropriate communication from the very beginning and reinforcing it along the way is vital.

Going hand in hand with this is to make sure that staff understands that they need to bring back to the manager any requests that a council member would make to them. Further, that their response to the council member must be that they will bring their request to the attention of the manager.

Be careful what you ask for, you may get it

Councils can be very clear in communicating their wishes for direction to a manager. However, it may be without a clear understanding of what they are asking or what the consequences may be. The Greenville City Council told the search firm they wanted a manager that would be a leader for developing the city. As much as I always tried to give credit to the mayor and council, the reality is that people saw me as the agent of the city's development. Of course, that was not my message or what either the council or I wanted, but it still led to some unhappiness. The same can often be said for changes the council may be supporting without recognizing there would be consequences to those changes. It becomes an even bigger problem for the manager when the council suddenly develops amnesia about ever asking for the change, *caveat vendor,* seller beware. While the seller (the council) should beware, the manager can be left holding the bag.

Taking over from an interim

This might not have been included had I not followed an interim in six of my professional positions, (two department director and four chief executive positions) five of whom then reported to me. Given those experiences and the challenges that can be presented, it seemed beneficial to include some thoughts on this type of situation. Four of the five times where the interim then worked for me, they had wanted the position and I was hired. Twice it worked out just fine, once was ok and the other two times (I need to use a technical management term here), it sucked.

As much as you think you can reach out to someone, show great respect and consult with them, if someone cannot deal with being passed over, it is going to be uncomfortable at best. Really professional people who understand why they were not selected can be fine but beware of the disgruntled employee who harbors resentment towards you. In the two situations where the former interim could not deal with the outcome, I really cut them a lot of slack and did everything I could do to bring them on-board. One was when I assumed a county administrator role and he did everything he could to undermine me. If I had to do it all over again, I would ask for their resignations as they were literally, cancers for the organization.

What is your opinion?

In so many ways, city or county managers cannot freely express their personal beliefs about things which do indeed matter to them. Managers are expected, and rightfully so, to be politically neutral. Given our positions and responsibilities, it really can be no other way. But it really does not stop with politics with a big P. It is all things that could have political undertones, including being in support of certain positions which would likely brand the manager as supporting one political ideology over another. To support gay marriage in the 1990s could have certainly alienated some council members. That could be true for loads of issues. Until retiring from being a local government manager, I felt I could not have an opinion on so many important matters of our times. My message is that is just the way it is, managers just need to live with it. And, there will be a day, when you indeed can freely express yourself. Believe me, you will still know how to do it!

So there are indeed quite a number of potential pitfalls to look out for as a manager. Being sensitive to individual council member concerns and recognizing their frustrations with the lack of their authority as an individual council member is critical. As indicated, it sometimes only takes one or two council members to sour a council on the manager. Understanding how to negotiate through what seems like intractable problems and "getting to yes" is a vital skill. Recognizing the challenges in being a change agent is also important as is effectively managing your level of visibility and taking over from an interim who ends up working for you. Finally, remember that you will have an opportunity to freely express your opinions on politics and sensitive public issues after you are no longer a manager.

This chapter has described many of the challenges of being a city/county manager. This theme will be continued in this next chapter which discusses organizational growth and change.

Chapter Seven

Organizational Growth and Change

Volumes of material have been written about organizational change. This chapter will not attempt to duplicate that wealth of information and excellent advice. Rather, it will focus on some significant aspects of the change process.

As important as what you are doing to change a local government's operation is how you do it. If you do not involve people in the organization, you will very likely fail in bringing about effective change. There are lots of ways of engaging people, but it must be genuine and give them a true opportunity to participate in a meaningful way. In addition, you must carefully gauge the pace of change in bringing the organization along. Finally, communication is absolutely essential. In the absence of knowledge, people will speculate and assume the worst outcome and the organization can almost shut down. Critical changes that cities or counties need often involve more than just the structure of the organization but also its culture. Organizations can become overwhelmed with the amount of change or constant change.

Staff involvement

When becoming the County Administrator for Hennepin County, I came to an organization that was as siloed as any could be. The county was divided into groupings, referred to as bureaus. Each was led by one of five assistant county administrators. In describing this situation, I usually say that the word "bureau" is indeed the root of the word "bureaucracy". The culture was calcified, and the ingrained practice was to work solely within your department and if communication outside the department occurred it was only as far as a department within the bureau and proceeded up the chain through department directors and virtually never across the organization to a peer in another department.

In any organization this would be dysfunctional, but the nature of the services the county delivered heightened the difficulty. About 75% of the services the county provided were human services, including public assistance, children and family services, mental health, public health and incarceration as well as medical services provided in a large 1000 bed hospital. A significant amount of the clients of each department were also served by other departments, with almost no coordination of the services.

In some ways, one can understand how this came to be. To begin with, communication and cross departmental work are tough with an organization with 10,000 people. Add to that, in the 25-year history of the county administrator form of government in Hennepin County prior to my arrival, there had been two administrators and the second one had served as the deputy administrator during the tenure of the first manager. The common practice was if a department director had an issue, they would just go up to the 23rd floor where the administrator had his fortress and be told what to do. As an aside, one of the things I did early on as the administrator is to knock down one of the two walls guarding the entrance to the county administrator's domain and put a glass wall on the second which looked into the office area. I also put a glass panel looking into my personal office. Of course, given the rumors of what previously happened on the couch (which had to go as well) in the administrator's office, the glass panel could have been a problem in the past!

It was clear that a very different approach to managing and integrating the organization was necessary. After much thought and discussion with the assistant county managers, we developed a matrix management concept. We would abolish the bureaus and assign each of the assistant administrators a functional responsibility which crossed the entire organization. They would orchestrate that responsibility using all the resources of the organization. The administrator, assistant administrators and department directors would all make up the Cabinet and the functional leadership team for the county. Since it would be impractical for the county administrator to have personnel responsibility for the entire cabinet, each department director was assigned to report for guidance and evaluation to an assistant manager and the assistant managers were all responsible to the manager.

Because this was such a large change from the way the county had been operating, it was essential to involve all the assistant managers and department directors during the development of this plan. I remember talking with one of the assistants who was struggling with how this would work. I took a step back and said that while we were considering this, we would not move forward if he did not think it would be effective and we would consider other approaches. However, if we did go forward, I asked him to think about how he believed it should work. He came back to me the next morning all excited with a plan of how he felt it would work for us to implement the structure we had envisioned. Involving him and others was critical.

Pace of change

There is a natural dichotomy that on one hand makes it important for change to occur fast enough for people have certainty that they will be ok or at least know what their new roles and responsibilities will be, who they will report to or what department they may be in. There is also an opposing need to pull back on the speed of the change process, slowing it enough that people can be involved, understand the transformed organization and the logic behind it.

When joining Hillsborough County as an Assistant County Manager, my responsibilities included all the departments responsible for planning, development, codes administration and permitting as well as engineering, capital project planning, design and construction. In particular, my charge was to shepherd the development and adoption of a comprehensive plan and system of development regulation that would meet the stringent growth management regulations adopted by the state legislature two years earlier as well as guide the planning, design and construction of a five year, one billion dollar capital improvement program. The county had passed a water and sewer bond issue of close to $500 million two years before my arrival with very little progress in building a system of water treatment and distribution as well as regional wastewater treatment and collection system. Not only was the clock ticking on spending the bond funds, but the environmental agencies were requiring quick action to replace some 200 interim wastewater treatment plants that were spread all over the county to handle its rapid growth.

Prior to my arrival there was little organizational capacity to deliver on these programs. Upon assuming my position I felt like it was not the County Administrator, Larry Brown, describing these challenges to me but Mr. Phelps on the tape that was going to self-destruct after listening to it. Clearly, there was a need for significant organizational change, and I did not have years to get going on this version of *Mission Impossible*.

116

Fortunately, Larry was a tremendously supportive County Administrator and believed in delegation.

Over the first several months, I worked with the department directors and others to fashion an organization which could deliver on the charge I was given. This involved a significant rearranging of staff responsibilities and departmental restructuring. Quite naturally, a major reorganization like this can create a great deal of anxiety. People not only want to know what will happen but also want to be able to provide their input. In order to get to a measure of certainty, decisions needed to be made in a timely fashion, creating the need to move relatively quickly as mentioned above. Yet we moved slow enough to involve others in the process. When coaching others about the change process, I always talk about the critical importance of the pace of change.

Pace is also important as people can only absorb so much change without shutting down. Larry Brown loved to be a change agent. He had come to the county a year before me and had moved forward with a series of major changes to the overall structure of the county and how business was done. Many of these changes were long overdue. However, it became overwhelming for the organization by the time of Reorg IV. We Assistant Managers had to go to Larry (one of my best bosses ever, by the way) and call a timeout.

Communication

Due to the scope of change in Hillsborough County, it was absolutely paramount to have open, frequent and in-depth communication throughout the ten departments and approximately 1,000 people involved. We established a newsletter that came out weekly or more frequently if there was something that needed to be communicated to the staff. I held a series of luncheon brown bag sessions throughout all the places that the departments occupied. I also instituted an open-door policy for anyone who wanted to come in and talk with me and did meet with quite a number of staff members.

Cultural change

Organizations are more often in need of cultural change than change in organizational structure. Through historical, control oriented management practices or sheer neglect, the initiative of employees can be stifled along with their creativity. Employees can feel devalued and that their contributions are not appreciated. Management practices sometime either promote or allow people's biases to affect personnel decisions and action. Those biases can take many forms including racial, ethnic or gender based. Those biases need to be dealt with directly and rooted out with a policy of zero tolerance.

The Minneapolis area was dominated by the settlement of Europeans of Scandinavian, Irish, German and Italian descent. The migration of African Americans was slow to reach all the way to the Twin Cities. While the area is becoming more diverse, the culture is dominated by Caucasians from Europe. This was certainly reflected in the leadership structure of Hennepin County at the time of my arrival in 1993. To their credit, the County Board of Commissioners recognized the need to diversify the leadership which at the time was almost entirely white males.

We undertook an aggressive recruitment effort to enhance the candidate pool for key positions which were available to be filled. We were successful in getting a diverse group of very qualified candidates in the groups of applicants for these positions and of the first 12 appointments to leadership positions, 9 were women or persons of color. To me the highlight of this success was the appointment of Dr. David Sanders to be the Director of Children and Family Services. Although David had some great experience and was highly qualified, he was relatively young and looked even younger. I felt that, for whatever reason, this African American had been overlooked for promotion. We elevated him two levels to the director position. David was a star and amazing Department Director. He went on to run the mammoth Los Angeles County Children and Families Department, the largest county system in the country and later received an appointment to a key administrative post by President Obama.

While cultural change can involve highly visible issues, it can also be more subtle, yet still important. As the Executive Director of the Maricopa Association Council of Governments (MAG), I had a large portion of the staff that were highly technical. These staff members ran the sophisticated transportation models for this large region in addition to doing all the air quality modeling using the complicated US Environmental Protection Agency highly technical programs. In order to obtain enough qualified computer modelers, MAG employed many people from foreign countries. I certainly learned a lot about US Immigration rules, Green Cards and H1-B Visas during my tenure with MAG.

As part of our effort in emotional intelligence, which will be described in a later chapter, we gained an understanding of how employees perceived our managers. To our surprise, we learned that most of the foreign nationals felt that they were not as appreciated as their American counterparts. While there was no discernable difference in pay, benefits or assignments, their perception of not being as valued was real.

In order to address this, I felt like we needed to celebrate the cultural diversity of the employees and highlight the interesting features of their different cultures. We established a series of luncheon presentations that employees gave on their cultures. We gave them time during work to prepare, although most did not take advantage of this and did most of the work after hours. We also gave them a budget to buy food for them to use in preparing some of their native dishes for the staff to sample. For the first of the luncheons, all the staff members that were available attended. For the second one, everyone who had a previous commitment changed their schedules to be able to be at the luncheon. It only took a few lunches for the foreign-born staff members to recognize that everyone valued them for who they were. Not only did this change their feeling of being valued but it brought the staff together and greatly enhanced the teamwork.

Obviously, the structure of an organization and how business is done are directly related. However, organizational restructuring will accomplish very little if the procedures for doing work stifles employees' enthusiasm. There are plenty of rigorous programs aimed at improving employee performance and I will not add to the literature describing them. However, beware of all the incremental decisions that can negatively affect employee initiative. If you are advocating the power of employees to make decisions on their own, you need to follow through on delegating the authority. Resist from making exceptions to this delegation. This includes procedures that centralize authority and take decisions out of the hands of individual departments. I have seen managers, out of concern for the proliferation of mobile phones, require all phones to be approved by the manager, even in large organizations. This often occurs in organizations where cost of telecommunications is budgeted at the organization level not the department level. Place the cost at the department level and make them live within their means and you will not only control the cost but also the number of phones.

Organizational downsizing

It is inevitable if you are in local government long enough you will need to go through the challenge of downsizing an organization. As I write this book, the country is going through one of our most difficult times in generations with the COVID-19 pandemic. The tremendous personal toll this will take on our citizens is not yet known. It is also hard to project the economic fallout from the drastically reduced business activity. However, it is clear that there will be very difficult financial times for our state and local governments. I can remember so vividly returning from the annual

ICMA conference in 1989 and at an airport seeing news of the stock market crash that led ultimately to the need for city and county cutbacks. Fiscal challenges returned with a vengeance in 2008 with the great recession.

Managing a city or county through a time of reducing budget and staff is an important duty of a manager. The importance of engaging staff and communicating during these times is vital. Again, much excellent guidance has been provided in professional literature on managing this process. I did want to describe one critically important strategy that does not seem to get enough mention.

While the Hennepin County Administrator, the board of commissioners asked me to rather dramatically cut the county's budget. The budget, staff and tax rate had grown significantly prior to my arrival and there was a strong belief that this growth needed to be substantially trimmed. In the annual proposed budget we presented we were able to reduce spending by millions as well as eliminate 500 funded positions. However, we were able to manage the cutbacks in a way that resulted in no layoffs of employees. We established a rigorous process that moved employees whose positions were being eliminated to other vacant positions that were funded. Granted, we had 10,000 positions but this cut was still 5% of the total staff complement.

The human resources department worked with all employees in positions that were being eliminated to identify their skill set and give them options for other positions which matched their backgrounds. Employees were given the option of applying for the available positions. In doing this is it is important to note that we looked at positions countywide and not just department by department. We established a procedure for reviewing each employee interested in an available position and giving the department director input in the selection process.

Going into this process we were able to reduce the fear and anxiety of employees by guaranteeing no layoffs and that they would have access to another position which matched their skill set. Knowing that we would be able to accommodate virtually everyone, we felt comfortable making this promise. We also established real time reporting of the status of filling these positions. While many cities and counties have gone through a process to place people in available positions, they often have not done so with a rigorous process which adequately handles employee placement.

We were successful in placing everyone that had to be moved to another position. There were a few employees that decided they would leave the county for other opportunities. Of course, you cannot always please everyone. One of the more liberal commissioners, although he voted for the budget, was not in favor of all the cuts and remarked at the adoption that I had given that budget screwdriver just a bit more of a turn than he would have preferred. My assistant county managers picked up on this and presented me with a rather unique gift. It was a screwdriver mounted on a plaque that read, "Bourey's Budget Screwdriver".

How much is too much

The amount or speed of change in an organization can be overwhelming. While the change in Hillsborough County was extensive, it was necessary and proved to be very effective. We built the one billion dollar capital improvement program. We adopted a plan and system of development regulations that resulted in the county being the first coastal county to have an approved growth management plan and regulatory system. In fact, we established an automated system to manage permitting to ensure "adequate public facilities" were in place prior to a permit being issued for development, which won an innovation award from the Harvard Kennedy School of Government. I thought that was really cool. Of course, not everyone was happy as it appeared that someone who was less than thrilled, twice keyed my car. After the second incident, I did wait to get it repaired until we were well beyond the restructuring.

So, I believe the change in Hillsborough County was not beyond what the organization could absorb, and it worked. Looking back to Hennepin County, I have to feel differently. While the changes in the structure of the organization may have been appropriate, the concept was so very different from the way the county had been operating, it was hard for many to understand and accept the changes as necessary. The culture of the organization did undergo a transformation and innovative approaches flourished. However, there were many dissenters and clearly some were not on board. It is hard to know if a less extensive approach would have produced as much energy and creative thinking but there certainly would have been less turbulence.

Thus, while the process of instituting organizational change can be difficult, there are actions that can help the process be successful. The following were suggested in this chapter:

- Communicating frequently and openly with those affected

- Maintaining a pace of change that is deliberative enough allow the opportunity for input, yet quick enough to give people certainty on the outcomes for them personally

- Not instituting too great of a change too quickly that it will overwhelm the organization

- Instituting a rigorous process to place employees into vacant positions where their positions are eliminated in a downsizing

- Recognizing the obstacles to change the culture of the organization and be sure to demonstrate the value of employees and be consistent with the commitments to delegate authority and responsibility

The ability to manage growth and change is vital for everyone in the profession. Also critical is working with the community. It is essential for the work local government professionals do. The next chapter explores this important dimension.

Chapter Eight

Community Involvement is Critical

An earlier chapter contains my perspective on the challenge of a city or county manager having a highly visible presence in the community. Regardless of whether the manager has a high profile or not, the manager and organization need to be in tune with the community and engaged in a variety of ways. While being very involved in many of the places I have worked, I was certainly more engaged in the Greenville community than any other place. That engagement had significant benefits but was also personally very rewarding. During my 10 years in Greenville, I was an active Rotarian and quite involved in our church. My activity as a United Way Board member and in the annual campaign, including serving as the Campaign Chairman after leaving the City Manager position, was especially fulfilling.

This involvement in Greenville gave people in the city an opportunity to see the city manager giving back to the community and committed to make a difference personally. It helped to establish me as one of them and a part of something beyond my work as the manager. The highlight of this service was chairing the Annual United Way Campaign for Greenville County. This was a huge team endeavor with a great volunteer and staff effort. To be able to play a significant role in a campaign that eclipsed $16 million and set a new state record for a local annual campaign was one of the most gratifying things I have ever been involved with.

Ironically, my volunteer work with the United Way and other community groups put me in contact with business and community leaders. For a number of years, I was responsible for leading the portion of the United Way Campaign for the 25 largest businesses. This got me fairly well acquainted with many of their leaders. Ultimately, this played a role in my recruitment by a number of private businesses when it was announced I was leaving the city manager post. This was the furthest thing from my mind when I was the manager and volunteering, but there was clearly an unintended benefit. Ironically, that volunteer engagement made me more valuable to private companies.

My involvement in a unique church community was also very fulfilling and will give a bit more insight into the city. St. Anthony of Padua was billed as, "a Catholic Church in the African American tradition". When hearing this description, my wife and I were not exactly sure what that meant. St. Anthony's was a Franciscan Mission Church in one of the poorest areas of the city. It had historically been an African American Church. However, others from outside of the church's immediate neighborhood discovered the sense of community, the warmth of the congregation and the tremendous energy of the parish. During the time we were part of St. Anthony's, the congregation dramatically changed as Caucasians began to attend in increasing numbers. They were all welcomed by the long time members. My wife has questioned more than once that if the tables were turned would the Caucasians have been as welcoming?

We were concerned that what made the church so special might be overwhelmed by the influx of people from outside the traditional congregation. Of course, we were one of them as well. While we had this concern, we also saw the value to the local community of the growth in the congregation. With the resources that the new arrivals brought in, the church was able to do amazing things. When we started to attend, the weekly collections were generally less than $2,000. Before we left they had increased more than 10 fold and were over $20,000. In addition, there were annual pledges well beyond what could have been imagined. Much of the credit for this growth and the benefits it provided needs to go to the dynamic and passionate Franciscan pastor, Father Patrick Tuttle.

St. Anthony's was very engaged in providing housing opportunities for community residents with very little resources. This was particularly crucial with the gentrification growing out of the successful redevelopment efforts. In addition, the resources of the church were used to feed many in need in the neighborhood.

The parish had operated an elementary school for decades. The school building was marginal at best and really needed to be replaced. We undertook a fundraising campaign and built a new $6 million school. One of my roles in this effort was to help sheppard through the use of New Market Tax Credits to help fund the construction. I will talk later about this federal program. It was experiences like this that made leaving Greenville so very difficult for us.

Many of the plans and programs of cities and counties require an active involvement of people in the community. Whether it is a comprehensive plan, a proposed major development or a major transportation project, obtaining citizen input is vital. Getting citizen input can be fairly easy if there is a controversial project that might have a major impact on a residential area. It can be a little more challenging for a long-range comprehensive plan that may not have an immediate impact. However, I think cities are getting better at reaching out to people and finding ways to engage them. Taking advantage of modern communication technology has been a significant assistance.

Community engagement can take many forms. While in Seattle, my department was working on the further development of the Burke Gilman Trail. Largely consisting of one of the early rails to trails projects, this was destined to become part of an amazing trail network circling Lake Washington with many feeder trails. We were meeting some resistance from many property owners adjacent to the prospective trail. In order to overcome this and work with the property owners, we did a survey of the property values along similar existing trail segments. We found that property values in an area *increased* the closer homes were to the trail. That study really helped to overcome some resistance. Admittedly, I was not a disinterested party in the trail development since I ran on that trail every morning back in the 80s when living in the city. When we moved back to the Seattle area last year, we located, as before, not far away from the trail. Once again using the trail, I am amazed at the housing investment next to the trail, with houses worth many millions of dollars that access the trail through their front or back yard. While these houses also have a great view of Lake Washington and the Cascades, other houses that do not share that trail access are not as opulent as the ones that do.

Newport News' One City Marathon

I would like to also illustrate the value of an effective community outreach program with a story about a major new event we launched in Newport News. The City of Newport News is very long and narrow. It is at most seven miles wide and about 25 miles long. The city originated with a relatively small four-square mile area which included the historical downtown. This is currently at the very southern end of the city. Largely through a combination with Warrick County, the city expanded to its current 120 square miles, about 50 of which is covered by bodies of water.

128

What has resulted is a city made up of districts and neighborhoods that are fairly separate, making a somewhat disjointed city.

The length of the city, close to 26 miles, and the desire to unify the city led to the notion of running a marathon from one end to the other. The idea of a marathon was actually suggested to me by a friend I was visiting with who lived in the Boston area while attending the 2013 ICMA Annual Conference. You already know I am an avid runner and marathoner, so, needless to say, I loved the idea of starting a marathon in the city. I was not exactly sure how people back home would respond to the idea. Much to my pleasure, the mayor and council as well as the staff were very supportive.

The concept I pitched was a marathon that would serve to help unite the community. We would run through many of the neighborhoods and finish downtown running through the Victory Arch, a monument first erected in 1919 as a memorial to those who served in the American armed forces. At this finishing site would be a big community party with bands, food and drink. In addition to unifying the city, this was also an attempt to encourage people to go downtown which had seen a mass exodus of activity. The race was dubbed the *One City Marathon* to emphasize the uniting mission.

Running a 26.2 mile race through an active city can be very disruptive. We needed to conduct the race on a Sunday to minimize conflicts with automobile traffic. This brought about another potential conflict with church services. Newport News is a very religious community with a great many churches; sometimes it feels like there is one on every street corner. With careful consideration of the disruptions as well as the most desirable places to run, we designed an awesome course. For anyone who wants to run a qualifying time for the Boston Marathon, this is a fast route and being run in March generally provides cool temperatures perfect for your qualifying attempt.

With that marketing pitch behind us, let's get to the challenge of working with the communities and churches to gain acceptance of carrying out a race that could cause much conflict. We knew that an early and active engagement plan was essential. I need to give a shout out to Telly Whitfield who was at the time the Assistant to the City Manager, for his great leadership in working with the community. We met people in their neighborhoods when it was most convenient for them to meet.

Not only did we get a level of cooperation, we got great enthusiasm. We established water stations each mile of the race that community groups could sponsor and assist with dispensing water to the runners. We established a contest for the best neighborhood support. The churches not only cooperated but some even changed the times of their services and came out to support the runners. What could have been a very disruptive situation became a community event and happening. So much of this success was due to a very active community engagement effort.

We had invited Boston Marathon Director Dave McGillivray to consult with us on the race and then run it with us. Dave has been an advisor on tons of marathons, and we were honored to have him participate. He told us that we had the most fan and community participation of any first-time marathon that he had ever been involved with. We were also told by many of the out of town participants that this was the friendliest marathon that they had ever run.

We gave Dave bib number one to honor his presence. I settled for number two. Since I introduced it to the City, I really did have to run it! I was very happy Dave was there even though I would have placed in my age group had he not finished ahead of me! I was fine coming in fourth in the 60 plus grouping. While I had run my first marathon more than 30 years earlier in Oklahoma in 3 hours and 15 minutes and this was over an hour slower, it was a very satisfying run.

Another intended benefit of this marathon was to help residents feel better about the city. Due to a variety of reasons, some look down on the city, sometimes referring to it as Newport Badnews. Newport News has had a relatively strong manufacturing history particularly with Newport News Shipbuilding which employs around 30,000 people. However, many view the city as a blue collar town with significant crime. This gave residents a chance to show off many of the city's special assets and boast about an outstanding event.

Dave McGillivray and me after the race

It does look like I am having fun running the One City Marathon

Newport News Police involved shooting

Community engagement is vital for so many city services, but nowhere is it more important than in policing of a city. This has been so clear with the series of high profile police involved shootings where race was a major issue. We had such an incident in Newport News and community involvement was critical in avoiding the negative community reaction, including violent protest and rioting, that has accompanied these situations in other cities around the country.

At about 1:00 a.m. on a Fourth of July morning, three police officers had an encounter with an African-American who possessed an illegal sawed off shotgun. This event took place in a dominantly African-American area of the city. I will not go into the particulars of the shooting but just say that the shooting was ruled to be justified by the officer who had shot the individual. This was after a lengthy and thorough investigation by not only the police department but by the independent prosecuting attorney's office.

Despite the circumstances of the shooting, many rumors circulated through the community. It was rumored he did not have a weapon, even though a weapon was present. It was falsely rumored that the individual was not threatening the police and they did not have to shoot. Regardless of the situation, community tensions can be raised under these types of situations.

Fortunately, the police chief, Rick Myers, was an outstanding professional who had experience with these types of issues. In a later chapter, I describe the hiring process we went through to select him as the city's chief. Chief Myers had been the chief in a number of cities, including serving as the interim chief for 11 months in Sanford, Florida after the Travon Martin shooting. He also had been brought in by federal authorities to coach other communities which faced similar volatile incidents, including Ferguson, Missouri.

From the beginning of his tenure, Chief Myers had reached out to build a level of trust with the African-American community. He had started a positive community dialog and made progress in bridging a gap that existed between the police and the community. In addition to the chief's outreach, Mayor Price, who I described earlier, also had great relationships in the community and this area, where he resided. Two other African-American council members also lived in the area.

When the incident occurred, the mayor and chief immediately reached out to the community. In particular, they connected with a group of the African-American ministers that provided a principal leadership role in the area. They were trusted by many who were members of the community. Not only did the mayor and chief appeal for calm but they also asked for patience while the investigations proceeded. In addition, they shared what information they could that would not compromise the inquiry.

As you would expect, the media was all over this and pushed hard to get everything they could. In order to be proactive, engage the media, provide as much up-to-date information as possible and limit the spread of rumors, I asked the chief to schedule a weekly media briefing. The mayor and council were invited to this press event and the mayor kicked off each presentation. I generally talked about non police matters relating to our effort to engage with the community. The chief went over as much of the details of the incident as he could divulge and updated people on the investigation. We answered all the questions with as much information as we could provide.

Despite attempts by a few members in the community that wanted to push their negative personal agenda, the community stayed calm during this process. The positive outreach before and after the shooting was critical to maintaining calm. I also think the very concerted effort to provide all the information we could kept the media satisfied and held down speculation about the circumstances which could have inflamed the situation. The importance of hiring outstanding professionals was never more evident than in this circumstance. In addition, the importance of a mayor who is willing to engage the community proactively and support staff was critical.

In summary, community involvement is critical on a personal level as well as that of an organization. The manager's engagement in civic and charitable efforts helps the community understand the values and integrity of the manager as well as build valuable connections. The early and encompassing outreach to segments of the community can spell the success or failure of an event or project.

This chapter has explored various aspects of working with the community. Working with another important group, the media, will be dealt with in the subsequent chapter.

Chapter Nine

Dealing with the Media

Over the course of my 43 year career, I have had a great deal of interaction with all types of media. By and large, I have had great relationships with television and newspaper reporters and received very favorable coverage. However, there have been a few reporters that have created great difficulty. I endeavor to not let those few ruin my experience and views of those that do a good job at their craft, but it is a struggle. As always, this chapter will not be a comprehensive guide on dealing with the media, but rather, it will offer some potentially valuable approaches.

I have found it most helpful to establish a relationship with the reporters who will be covering the city or county issues prior to the need to deal with any sensitive issues. When arriving in town or even before, I have sought out a meeting to get to know them. I have felt that it was important to make sure they knew I value their work and felt they provide an important public service. My pledge was always to be as open as possible and provide all the information they wanted; of course, with the caveat that there would be times when I would be bound by confidentiality. I would say that my hope was that they understood it would be necessary at times to withhold certain information. I provided all my contact information including my mobile number. I rarely got late calls on mundane matters. It happened a few times but, it was worth the openness it showed. I always tried to provide an insight into why I was a manager and the importance I put on serving the public. Almost all reporters responded very favorably to this overture. Of course, there were a few sceptics and more than one downright cynic. But then I could find out upfront who to watch closely.

Some reporters will try to be confrontational and attempt to bait you into a conflict. They believe it is their job to be confrontational. While in Minnesota, I actually had a reporter doing a profile piece on me criticize me for going to employee funerals. Really? He said it was just not the Minnesota way. I continued that practice throughout my career and the family of the deceased was always so appreciative, as were other employees. It is important to avoid being drawn into conflict, it will just lead to more conflict and be a difficult spiral to get out of. I got into a very negative situation with a newspaper that will be described in a later chapter that pretty much cost me my city manager position.

There are a few ways that you can help to increase the odds that you will be at least somewhat accurately represented. If you are on the phone with a reporter, it is a bit difficult at times to know if they are getting it all down. I developed a practice of listening to their typing and making sure to go slowly, taking a bit of a break in speaking, until I could hear them stop typing. Then, I figured they were at least up to where we were in the conversation. It can be effective to do that in person as well. Make sure they are caught up in writing in their notepad. Otherwise you will be too far ahead, and they will not be able remember what you said.

I have always welcomed being recorded. Far from a threat, I considered it a bit of an assist in being accurately quoted. It also shows cooperation and an openness with them. It is more of a protection for you than a problem. Of course, that is true unless you say something really stupid; just don't do that! If you are particularly nervous about the ethics of a reporter, you can always tape it yourself as well.

Media trainers will almost always advise people not to go "off the record", as they feel that nothing is really off the record and you cannot be assured what you say won't be reported and will be attributed to you. I have gone off the record in certain instances to assist the reporter to get the story correct or even to have them back off something that may not be appropriate to report. I only did so when I had already developed a high level of trust with the reporter and if they did not honor it being off the record, it would not have created a big problem. Never go off the record with something that absolutely must remain confidential.

I am not a fan of having a "city spokesperson" under most circumstances. I have had some great public information officers but no matter how good they are, they will not know the issues like a professional that is deeply involved in the matter. I also think the public is often skeptical that spokespeople are sent when someone does not want to talk with the media. That is indeed true at times.

Be prepared for the reporters to not grasp all the details or finer points of an issue. And, be prepared for the editors who were not involved in the conversation to get things confused. I had an incident where the slight change of an article changed the meaning of a statement. While the Director of Community Development for Cherry Hill, I was addressing the requirement for our community to have our "fair share" of affordable housing. This was a mandate because of an interpretation of the State Constitution by the New Jersey State Supreme Court. I was explaining that we needed to comply because it was the law. It was reported that I said we needed to comply because it was a law. Well, there was some measure of controversy that the State Legislature had not dealt with this requirement. It was not a law but due to the court action it was the law. This did not end up being a big deal, but it is amazing how the change from a the to an a can change the meaning of a statement.

Give the media what they need

It is important to recognize that the media has a job to do and when you can help them accomplish their goals, you can establish an effective partnership with them. To illustrate this point, I will describe the circumstances when the City of Greenville sheltered evacuees from New Orleans as a result of Hurricane Katrina. This effort has many lessons, beyond dealing with the media, but the response to the media was critically important. Most all readers are likely to have knowledge of the massive and intense hurricane which hit the City of New Orleans and severely impacted coastal areas of Louisiana, Alabama, Mississippi and Florida on August 23, 2005. This was one of the most intense storms ever to hit the United States and certainly was among the costliest. The city was not able to be fully evacuated and the conditions were so severe that many had to be rescued by boat and helicopter from the city. After leaving or being rescued from the area, thousands of people were temporarily sheltered in many places throughout the southeast. Due to the difficult circumstances, many family members were separated and did not even know where their relatives were staying.

Knowing the tremendous difficulties that the city residents were facing and wanting to help, the City of Greenville Council wanted to assist in the sheltering of residents relocated from the hurricane ravaged area. The council asked me to investigate whether we could shelter some evacuees in our convention center. I investigated what it would take to do that and how we could get it done. The council instructed me to proceed with the sheltering approach that we developed.

As you would imagine, this required a very rapid response and most intensive effort. We felt it would be critical to involve many partners to provide as broad array of services and support to the evacuees as we could. These people were leaving their homes with very few personal belongings and minimal resources. We had to assemble all that they would need to live in our convention center. We acquired cots, bedding, toiletries and food, among other necessities. We set up lockers to house valuables. After 48 to 72 hours of frantic preparation we were ready to receive our first plane load. We were prepared to receive well over 1,000 evacuees and did end up housing several hundred. This was just the first of many 18 hour days for me as I personally directed the effort at the request of the council. So many staff members also put in extremely long days and did outstanding work.

As the passengers from New Orleans approached Greenville, they were told where they would be sheltered. Upon hearing they were going to be in Greenville, South Carolina, many wondered where Greenville was and what it was like. We felt it was important to be as welcoming as possible and make them feel comfortable in their stay. I was there with others as they arrived and told them that we would do whatever we could to meet their needs and make them as comfortable as we could.

We engaged multiple city departments and partnered with the county health and social services departments. We also involved state agencies. All the city, county and state agencies had offices established on site. We also located 50 computers with technical support staff to assist them in locating where other family members were located. We even had community volunteers, including my wife, come in to assist in finding relatives. We housed, fed and provided all other necessary support. This included assisting them in applying for federal benefits and setting them up with transportation, if they had alternate safe places they wanted to go. We bought plane and bus tickets to accommodate their travel. Virtually all of our costs would be reimbursed by the federal government.

There was a very strong community interest and the media was voracious in their appetite for information and to tell the stories of our guests. The local television and print media pressed for as much detail as possible and for direct access to the evacuees. We were faced with a real balancing act. While we wanted to be as cooperative as possible with the media representatives, the evacuees were basically living, sleeping and eating in this public facility. We could not give them free access to wander around the places where people were sleeping and making their temporary home. In addition, most of these folks had been through very harrowing experiences, including being airlifted from rooftops where they were stranded. Some were in pretty fragile states.

I decided we needed to have a daily media briefing to keep them all up to date with the number of the evacuees we were sheltering and the issues they were facing. We also provided a general viewing of the area once a day but did not permit them to go right up to guests. In addition, we asked if anyone from the evacuees would be ok talking with the media and we provided a time to make them available for interviews. The media responded very well to this approach and we received positive in-depth coverage by all the reporters. The community in general felt good about hosting these guests.

We also had quite a challenge with the religious community. A significant number of ministers wanted to contact the evacuees and bring them to their churches. They wanted free and continual contact with the residents. This came to a head in one particular meeting I had with a group of African American ministers who felt we were unfairly restricting their access. We worked at developing a fair plan to balance their interests and the privacy of the evacuees. I did not really know how much they respected us working with them until a few months later. While I was attending the annual meeting of the local chapter of the NAACP, I was surprised to receive the Coretta Scott King Humanitarian Award for my work with the Katrina evacuees. Many of the leaders of this chapter were the very ministers I dealt with during our sheltering effort.

Some of the people that came to Greenville stayed in the community. One of those was Mary, a woman who joined the congregation at St. Anthony's, where we attended. She was an inspiration for so many as she had been through very difficult times even prior to Katrina, losing family members to tragic circumstances. Yet she was always upbeat and thankful for what she gained in her new home.

Working proactively with the ministers' interest group was a valuable lesson from this effort. In the same way, working with the media and providing them with what they needed to do their jobs and tell the story was instructive. Also, involving a broad range of partners to provide a full range of services was critical for the success of the sheltering project. This was reinforced when the Federal Emergency Management Agency told us that this was the best run shelter that they had seen and we had provided the most complete spectrum of support services of any shelter.

This effort was one of the most gratifying I have ever been involved with. I remember feeling incredibly touched when saying goodbye to a group of guests and one said to me, "When we arrived and heard you say what you would do for us, we really did not believe you; but you were true to your word and you treated us with respect and dignity, made us feel welcome and did all you could to help us". It cannot get any better than that. That expressed thanks made the long days more than worth every minute!

Using the media

As much as the media can be frustrating at times, we need to remember that the media is critical for public information and managers can use it to their advantage. When serving as the MAG Executive Director, I dealt with a very thorny issue in which the media was instrumental to our success. Many years before my arrival in Phoenix, the county had passed a half cent sales tax to pay for a regional freeway system. The region had entered into the freeway building business relatively late because they took the position that if they didn't build a high capacity road network growth would not come. Don't build it and they won't come! No "freeway of dreams". The tax to build freeways was adopted when they woke up to the folly of their approach and growth was strangling the inadequate road network.

Over the years, after the tax was passed and prior to my arrival, the State Transportation Board had moved more and more of the federal and state gas tax collected in the region away from the Phoenix area to other parts of the state, figuring that the region had the sales tax money. This resulted in the region getting a small fraction of the gas tax dollars that were generated in the region. This happened, at least in part, because the State Transportation Board was made up of members that were predominantly from outside of the Phoenix area.

We identified this problem for the MAG Regional Council, and they directed me to undertake a campaign to reverse this outflow of funds. This description will not go into all the detailed strategy and plan to accomplish it. However, one of my efforts involved getting very engaged with the State Transportation Board to bring our case to them for a more representative distribution of the revenue. We felt it should more closely reflect where the money was raised. For quite some time I followed the board all over Arizona to their meetings. I would stay at the same places they stayed and break bread with them in the evenings. Suffice it to say that the board was inclined to just keep the distribution of funding the way it was since the areas they represented were getting much of the gas tax generated in the MAG area.

Part of our effort involved a media education campaign, particularly with the Arizona Republic newspaper. The paper jumped onto the cause and ran quite a number of articles about the inequity of the funding distribution. This included a great editorial with a series of pie charts (that we had produced for them) showing where the money was raised and where it was allocated. This publicity was absolutely a key to getting the State Transportation Board's attention. They not so subtly indicated that to me by producing a laminated copy of the pie charts which they used as a placemat for me at one of our dinners.

The result of this campaign and the publicity was the redistribution of $691 million dollars of funding over a five-year period from other parts of the state back to the Phoenix region. This enabled us to accelerate construction of the regional freeway system by seven years.

We were most fortunate that the Arizona Republic understood the importance of this issue and got the story correct. However, that is too often not the case. No longer being a city manager and particularly, not the Newport News City Manager, I can relatively freely describe an opposite situation. The daily newspaper that covers Newport News and is located in the city is the Daily Press. Commonly known as the Daily Depress or Daily Mess, the paper took every opportunity to be negative about the community and thwart most any efforts to build a better place. It was shocking that they actually wrote most positively about the One City Marathon. But then, we got them to sign on as a sponsor and have a vested interest.

Telling your own story

In addition to not getting stories correct, they would just not write anything or cover something well after it happened. It was not unusual for the paper to cover a major community event weeks after it occurred.

Out of utter frustration, I decided we needed to get our activities and stories out to our citizens. I asked the staff to develop a daily electronic newsletter. The one page newsletter would generally contain three short stories, a couple paragraphs in length with links to longer pieces and more detailed information. I know the thought of a daily newsletter freaked out the staff. However, the concept was to get the stories written by the departments. I came up with many of them and wrote them up initially. I felt it was critical for the residents to get used to a daily email and be thinking about it.

Through access to email addresses for at least one member of the city's households, we were able to start with a database of about 75,000 email addresses. Of course, we gave everyone an opportunity to opt out of the email. We did have about 5,000 opt out over the first few months but others joined.

Everyone will say that this has been an outstanding success. Residents are enthusiastic about it and the city has a vehicle to get great information to the public. I feel quite certain that it reaches many more Newport News households than the Daily Repress (whoops, yet another pet name). Hopefully, the reader knows it is a good-natured ribbing of this newspaper, well maybe… As you read a later chapter, you can draw your own conclusions.

Throughout most of my career, social media either did not exist or it played a relatively minor role in how people communicate with one another or get a message out to groups of people. The world is much different today. During the time I was the City Manager in Greenville, cities began to take advantage of Facebook as a way to communicate and some managers began to do daily or periodic blogs. I was always reluctant to do a personal blog and remained so through the remainder of my career as I felt it would be interpreted to be too much about the manager and me and not enough about all the employees of the city and what they do. It seemed that I always garnered too much attention already.

However, Facebook and later Twitter and other social media platforms are great ways to get out a city's message broadly and to groups that do not always pay attention to other media. When in Newport News, we sought out some relatively young folks to work in the public information department and gave them a pretty free hand at posting on Facebook and tweeting away. These proved to be great communications tools.

Indeed, while the media can be a source of frustration and agony, it is also critical to an open and democratic governance. This chapter pointed out some techniques that can help in working with the media, including:

- Establishing an early positive relationship with key reporters can help to build trust for future conversations

- Making sure the reporter is capturing what you say by going slow enough for the writing or typing to keep up

- Not going "off the record" unless you have a high level of confidence in the reporter and it is something that would not be a big problem if it was made public

- Avoiding being baited into a conflict if it is at possible

- Partnering with the media to get a story right

- Taking advantage of the fact that the media can be used as a tool in achieving success for certain projects

- Establishing the organization's own direct communication tool such as the Newport News daily email that was described

Effectively handling the media will always be an important skill for managers. Also vital is the ability to hire people who will be an excellent fit for the organization and excel in their job performance. This is the subject of the next chapter.

Chapter Ten

The Hiring Process

All managers know that the hiring and development of key people is as critical as anything you will do. Make a good hire and you will reap the rewards. Hire someone who is a bad fit for the position and organization, and it can haunt you for years. This chapter will contain a few of the approaches I found to be successful in helping to ensure that those brought on will be great for the city or county.

Asking appropriate questions to ensure candidates have the knowledge and skills to perform in the position you are hiring for is obviously important. However, I always have thought it is equally important to understand the motivation and real interest in working with the organization. Having someone who is committed to serving the public is critical. Intelligence, attitude, energy and willingness to learn are all vital to what they can contribute to the organization.

Getting to know the applicants in a personal way is important. I always seek an informal setting, such as a lunch meeting, to have a casual conversation. Over a lunch meeting and extended conversation, candidates will tell you things about themselves that you cannot legally ask or might not even know to ask. Of course, if the candidate is a real dud, the lunch will seem interminable. Even though there have been a couple of pretty long lunches, they all have been well worth the investment.

For senior level positions, I believe in an extended and challenging interview process. As a candidate, I have participated in some very arduous processes. I actually welcomed it as an opportunity to show my skills and abilities. There certainly do not appear to be as many candidates in applicant pools as many years ago when we baby boomers were regularly competing for jobs and more willing to relocate. The number of applications for the position I obtained with Hillsborough County was 500. While they were obviously not all well qualified, it was certainly a competitive situation. The county had several rounds of narrowing the field before bringing us in for interviews. This included asking the candidates to complete a series of essay questions. Please note, this was done in the process of narrowing the list, not with the initial application. I advocate doing this when winnowing the applicant list as you get some excellent information and can eliminate the casual applicant. With current technology, some people apply for jobs just to test the waters without a strong interest in accepting the position if it is offered. After narrowing the list, the interview was two long days of an assessment center and individual interviews.

The same was true for the Hennepin County selection process. They narrowed the field from about 150 to a smaller subset who were asked to write responses to questions. The group was then reduced to about a dozen who were brought in for a two-day assessment center. The next cut was to six and back to Minneapolis a third time for interviews. During that same trip, the candidates were reduced to three for final interviews and a selection. I then made a fourth trip to the county for a public confirmation vote by the board. Both Hillsborough and Hennepin Counties knew what they were getting by the time they selected me. The more rigorous you make the process, the more you will learn and the more likely that you will find the best fit. I recommend exposing people to different situations and settings.

In addition, I have always been committed to involving others in the search process both outside and inside the organization. This encompassed not only peers, but also potential subordinates including secretaries and receptionists. People have asked if I am concerned that the feedback will be all over the place and that people will have very different views on who should be selected. I have never ended up with that problem. Part of the reason is that people are asked not to rank candidates but rather give feedback on the strengths and weakness of the candidates.

To provide a context for this, I will describe the hiring process we followed in the selection of a police chief for both the Cities of Greenville and Newport News. In each case the field was narrowed to a group that was run through a professional assessment center to closely evaluate their professional skill sets. The field was then further reduced to five candidates for personal interviews. The interviews included the following:

- A panel of police department representatives

- The city department directors and assistant managers

- The entire police department

- The public

The night before the interviews, we held a dinner with all the candidates and their spouses along with the assistant managers, our spouses and me. The idea was to find out as much as we could about the candidates as well as share information about the community from multiple perspectives. After each of these sessions, I met with the groups interviewing the candidates and got feedback. We did a fairly similar procedure for the selection of a fire chief for Newport News.

Just prior to the dinner, we held a reception with the candidates, their spouses and council members. This was done as a courtesy although it was clear the council members would make some comments. In Newport News Council members are specifically prohibited from attempting to influence who the city manager will hire.

For high level positions, it is important to include the spouse/significant other in a recruitment process. It is not only the candidate that will have to approve the relocation decision. A story will serve to illustrate this point quite well. About 20 years ago, the City of Spartanburg, South Carolina was recruiting a city manager. Their top candidate was Mark Scott, who is now a friend who I enjoyed working with for several years. The Mayor was most anxious to get him to come to the city and interview. However, they had him come when his wife was not available. Mark was offered the position but declined as his wife had not seen the area. It would have been a major move as Mark was the Beverly Hills City Manager. Not only is Spartanburg a long way from Beverly Hills it is also culturally very different, as you would imagine.

The manager that was hired, did not last a long time. So, a couple years later, the Mayor made another run at Mark. This time, they scheduled a visit for both Mark **and** Carol Scott. When the mayor picked them up from the airport, he greeted Carol and had her sit in the front seat with him and Mark sat in the back. He knew Carol had to be convinced it would be good to relocate. Mark served as the Spartanburg City Manager for about the same time that I served in nearby Greenville. As it turns out the City of Greenville benefited from Carol's relocation as she was the first Executive Director of the Children's Museum of the Upstate located in Downtown

Greenville. She led the creation of the physical layout and was instrumental in development of the permanent exhibits.

There are also several procedural approaches I have found to be valuable. Some organizations like to wait on reference checks until a candidate is singled out. It seems more helpful to do reference checks before the interviews and have the benefit of that information as a selection is made. In addition, this avoids the problem that is created if someone has been selected and then something negative is discovered in their background. In addition, it is good to talk to people that know the candidate but are not on their reference list. Obviously, this needs to respect the candidate's desire for confidentiality.

It is also best to not close a recruitment before finalizing the selection. When leading a recruitment, I like to say on a posting that the first review of candidates will occur on a given date, generally 30 days after the initial date of advertising. That lets candidates know they have 30 days to get their application in or they may not be considered. This allows consideration of candidates that might apply afterwards and avoids needing to do another round of advertising and applications. It is also especially important to delay announcing a selection until you have a completed agreement. If some negotiation is involved, the city or county will be at a disadvantage if they have already announced who they want.

Hiring decisions can be difficult when there are qualified candidates that are both highly desirable. One of the most difficult decisions of any kind I made as a manager involved the hiring of an Assistant County Administrator for El Dorado County, California. The search came down between two highly qualified people. One of them was a good friend who I met when I first started to work as a professional and had stayed in touch with for 25 years (now 43 years). While he was a friend, the hiring decision obviously needed to be made based the best fit for the organization's specific needs. It crushed me to have to hire the other candidate. I still feel the pain of that decision. Fortunately, my friend did not hold that against me, and we are still friends today.

After hiring someone, I have always felt a responsibility to ensure they were successful. Out of the dozens of people that joined me, only one has not work out. I feel strongly that if you make the process very rigorous and engage others to help, you will not make a mistake. The one time misfire, there was something in his background that a former employer did not divulge and would have been hard to know without that information. He once again reverted to unacceptable actions that we could not tolerate.

This chapter describes a number of strategies to help ensure a successful hire. Below is a summary of those strategies.

- Look for someone that will have a commitment to the organization

- Put a premium on the candidate's intelligence, attitude, energy and willingness to learn

- As part of the interview process include a casual setting like lunch to learn about the candidate

- After screening for the best applicants, ask them to complete a series of essay questions to further narrow the list to determine who should be interviewed.

- Establish a very rigorous process for senior level positions including a thorough assessment

- Involve others, including their potential peers, staff and, where appropriate, the public in the interview process

- Invite the spouse/partner to the city along with the applicant and engage them in the process

- Do references checks before the final interviews

So, after the hiring decision, a manger must be effective in nurturing and guiding those brought on board. The following chapter describes the importance of this role.

Chapter Eleven

It's About We not Me

As I have said earlier in this book, what gets done in cities and counties is what gets done through staff actions. It is essential for the manager to be the leader for the organization's work. The effective manager will do this through setting expectations and delegating, nurturing and guiding assistant managers and department directors as well as building a team that can effectively work together and jointly manage the organization.

In setting expectations, I worked to provide the assistant managers and department directors an understanding of the following:

- Policy direction set by the city council

- Priorities for their actions

- Roles and responsibilities of assistant managers and department directors

- Standards of ethical behavior

- Importance of communication

- Need to keep me informed

- Nature of staff's relationship with the Council

Delegate everything you can

In starting a new position, I always tell people I am a totally dedicated delegator. I tell my team that means delegating *everything* possible. So many say that but really do not fully put it into action. My total commitment to investing responsibility to others probably comes as much from absolute necessity as much as the knowledge of it being what a manager must to do. As I gained increasing responsibility up to and including my position as the Hennepin County Administrator, I recognized that if the organization was going to accomplish an aggressive set of objectives, others needed to be fully engaged and do the work.

Even issues I needed to be familiar with could be delegated. The key was keeping me informed on things I needed to know. That comes from the people I work with having a clear understanding of the nature of what they need to tell me. That is the nature of items, not going over specific items. It is essential that everyone has a general understanding of what is important and be able to use their judgement. We employ people for not only their skill in technical and tactical work but also to have good judgement.

It is common in the profession to hear statements by managers similar to, "I delegate responsibility to staff and then get out of the way". Certainly I agree with delegating and giving responsibility but a manager also needs to support the staff by always processing requests and approvals in a timely manner. During the course of a day, a lot comes through the manager's office for delegation or action. Prior to the advent of so much electronic business, that used to mean a lot of paper. The larger the city or county, the more paper. When I was the Hennepin County Administrator, which measured as much as a two foot stack of paper every day. In Newport News, it was a lot of paper, but the emails were the killer. I would regularly get at least 200 each day.

As difficult as it was most days, my commitment to staff as well as myself, was to handle everything that came in during the course of the day, by assigning, approving or processing as appropriate. I was not going to delay work getting underway or stop a recommendation going forward. Of course, sometimes that meant sending something back to staff with questions. This was not easy to do but it was essential, not only to keep things moving but also to keep from being overwhelmed and then finding it virtually impossible to catch up. It made for some long days, but if something was not going to get done that day then when was it going to be done? At the end of the day, my goal was a **totally** empty in-box. I was once sitting beside a manager from a neighboring community at a meeting and in a casual glance at the iPad she was working on during the meeting saw that she had hundreds of unopened emails in her in-box. It sent a shiver down my spine!

This is made a lot easier if the manager has some time during the day to work on the daily processing requests. It is essential not to be so overbooked with meetings that there is no work time. Accurately judging how long a meeting is going to take and giving yourself sufficient time in transit when the meeting is out of the office is critical. You need to schedule for success.

Performance evaluations

I viewed my role as a manager as *leading* the organization not *managing* it. Leaders need to provide overall guidance for the work that is done. One needs to outline a vision and approach to doing work and then get out of the way. However, frequent and direct feedback is essential. People need to know how they are doing and be coached appropriately. Some of you may have heard the sort of response I received when asking a previous manager of my organization why he had not done performance evaluations. His response was, "I told people they did not need an evaluation because if they were not doing what they should be I would have fired them". Not two or three strikes but one strike and you are out. Very comforting!

Surely some of my human resources directors have been a bit frustrated with me totally ignoring the personnel evaluation forms they devised. I have a bit different idea of what evaluations should be like at a senior level of a city or county. Each assistant manager and department director should have a clearly delineated set of goals and objectives for the year. They need to be evaluated based on those agreed upon items. Prior to evaluating someone, I ask them to write up a summary of their accomplishments and how they did in meeting their goals and objectives as well as the things they need to focus on for the next year. Neither one of these things should be a surprise to them or me because we have continually stayed in touch and I have provided ongoing feedback. Of course, that is the plan, and nobody is perfect. I am sure I have not always been on top of this but rarely has either of us been surprised.

The evaluation meeting is really a conversation about the year and what they need to focus on going forward. It always starts with a recitation of the things that they did well and that I appreciate and then *we* talk about what they need to do going forward. Some of these conversations are not as comfortable as others if there is a performance issue, but people have always said they felt it was a good dialog and was constructive. We also talk about professional development. This includes the focus they have for their future and the professional development activities they should undertake.

I memorialize the meeting in a memorandum to them outlining all that has gone well and the agreed upon objectives for the following year. I am not advocating my way is the very best or what everyone should do, but it has worked well for me. The professional development part is critical. They need to know the organization cares about them and is willing to invest in them.

You will see in a number of places in this book I talk about investing in employees. I have indeed got pushback at times from some saying that we are just training people to be more valuable to some other city or county. To that, I say it is fine. We will try to keep them, and I believe showing people that we care about them as individuals will help them feel good about their jobs and where they work. If they leave, then we will have had dedicated and well-trained folks when they worked with us.

Letting an employee go

So what if you work with an assistant manager or department director over some period of time, setting expectations, coaching and giving feedback and then it becomes clear that they just are not a good fit for the position? If they prove to be very difficult to coach, display bad judgement, have a very poor attitude and are not committed to the organization, they just need to leave. If you feel like they could be coached and do not suffer from poor judgement or attitude and lack of commitment, yet consistently do not perform up to expectations, perhaps they could be moved to another position more in tune with their skill set. Either way, you really need to take action to either fire them or move them to a different position.

The conversation you have with someone you are firing or reassigning to a different position is critically important for the organization and the employee. Since you will have gone through a coaching and feedback process with them, firing or moving them should not be a surprise to them. If the person is a department director and reports to an assistant manager, the meeting would have been with the assistant manager and me. If the person reports directly to me, I would likely involve the human resources director to have a witness to the conversation. I really do not like to have any more than one other person in the room, as it just adds to the embarrassment for the employee.

When I have been in this situation, the conversation has generally started with a summary of where we were with their performance and leads to the conclusion that we must make a change. I go out of my way to say this is not about their value as a person and make sure they are shown respect. If there has not been a flagrant act that would warrant firing in and of itself, I would offer the employee the opportunity to resign. If it is someone with a fairly significant tenure, I would offer some severance for them, anywhere from a few weeks to three months. The offer is presented with a separation agreement that they need to sign right away. If they would not agree to sign within 24 hours, the agreement and severance is off the table. What I would present was non-negotiable. The separation agreement always included a clause for no negative comments or action against the organization and represents a final agreement with the employee. By law, they always have at least a week to retract their agreement.

If the employee is being moved to another position you must be assured that they will be positive and see it as an opportunity to stay with the organization. If not, they must go.

I have had to let go quite a number of people over the years; those that I inherited who just could not or would not adequately perform despite setting clear expectations, giving continual feedback and coaching. I have never had any further issue with an employee suing or taking any action against the organization. I did have a frivolous racial bias complaint from an employee who did not report directly to me that was judged by the Equal Employment Opportunity folks to be without merit. I also had an employee who was fired that harbored a lot of resentment and displayed that one night at a restaurant when he saw me by giving me the finger in front of dozens of people. Oh well, you cannot please everyone.

Developing an executive team

As important as it is to set expectations and delegate to assistant managers and department directors, it is also vital to develop them as a team, working together to lead the organization. In assuming some manager positions, I have been very surprised at how isolated the department directors were from one another. Earlier I described this situation in Hennepin County but it was also the circumstance in other places as well. When I assumed the city manager position in Newport News, I was astounded to learn that the department directors were only meeting on a quarterly basis. I felt like I almost had to introduce them to one another.

In Newport News, as in every place I managed, I established weekly meetings for the assistant managers and department directors. The meetings generally ran about an hour to an hour and one half and were an opportunity for each participant to share things going on in their departments that were important for the group to know. I felt that enough happened over the course of a week that going longer than that without meeting would be problematic.

These meetings developed a level of familiarity with one other. It also developed a broader knowledge for each of the directors of what was going on in the city. Many directors would regularly come in contact with the public and would be asked about situations beyond their departments. Having some level of knowledge about other departments could be very helpful. It was also valuable to bring up and discuss issues that other departments were facing. Putting many heads together to solve issues is so much better than relying on just one person. And that goes for the manager as well. Consulting with others can greatly improve the decisions a manager makes.

In addition to these meetings, I always held semi-annual retreats of this group. These were off site sessions generally a day and a half. These meetings included professional development activities such as emotional intelligence training, strategic planning sessions and team building activities. We all ate together and spent some personal and relaxed time with each other. I generally always facilitated these retreats, although we did bring in some outside resource people when it would benefit the session. I feel strongly that going somewhere to stay overnight and eating meals together provides an excellent break from the norm and greatly enhances interaction. It also builds strong interpersonal relationships and trust among team members. This does translate to a more cohesive team effort.

This chapter has stressed the importance of setting expectations, delegating and the criticality of developing the leadership team through coaching, guiding and providing regular feedback. In particular, it describes a positive and constructive performance evaluation process. The chapter also outlined important considerations in letting an employee go if they are not going to work out. It also has described some methods to help build an effective team.

Just as managers need to nurture employees, they need to be able to build effective relationships with the private sector. This important facet of local government management will be addresses in the following chapter.

Chapter Twelve

Public Private Partnerships

In the next few chapters, the book will focus on substantive topics of managing cities and counties. These are topics where my experience seems to offer a perspective that is beyond traditional management literature. As always, this is presented from the bias of my experience and what has been successful. These start with public private partnerships because so much of what happens in a community comes through these partnerships. Cities and counties generally do not develop properties for housing, commercial or industrial uses. However, those developments do not happen without public infrastructure to support the sites and buildings. Often, cities and counties take the strategy of encouraging economic development by providing incentives for the private sector in addition to providing public infrastructure. While there can be some disagreement on the use of these incentives, most informed participants in this process will agree that incentives can sometimes make a difference in whether or not some valuable development takes place.

So, when is an incentive for development appropriate and when should the public sector not provide an extra boost for development? How much is just enough and how much is more than is necessary? Let's explore these issues with a story involving a sports facility. There is often significant controversy on incentives for sports teams to relocate to or keep them from moving away from an area. To many, it seems that some professional sports teams have almost held a community hostage with demands for public investment in stadiums and arenas to keep a team from relocating or to attract a team to move into the city.

Minor League Baseball

This story begins when I arrived in Greenville, South Carolina as the city manager. The Atlanta Braves baseball team had owned and operated a AA Minor League baseball team in Greenville for more than 20 years. For those that may be unfamiliar with how Minor League Baseball works, most Major Leagues teams do not own and operate their own farm teams. Rather, they sign what is referred to as a player development agreement with another entity that owns and operates the Minor League Team. The Atlanta Braves are one of the exceptions and operate all their own Minor League teams.

For more than 20 years, the Braves farm team played in a stadium owned by the city. It was about five miles outside of downtown on the outskirts of the city, but still in the city limits, in a fairly industrial area without many surrounding commercial uses, certainly none that would support the baseball game experience. This stadium was very outdated and would have cost a great deal to renovate to present day standards. Moreover, its location was hardly ideal. The city council was particularly interested in locating a stadium in the downtown area to help contribute to the revitalization of the downtown, which needed an additional boost.

During my research on city issues, building a new baseball stadium and retaining the Atlanta Braves AA team was identified as an important goal of the city. This was a reasonably comfortable task for me as I had previously been engaged in negotiations with Major League Baseball teams. While serving as the Senior Assistant Manager for Hillsborough County, I had worked with the Boston Red Sox and New York Yankees on the location of their spring training facilities into the county. For full disclosure I need to divulge that I was raised and lived until middle school in the New England states and am a diehard Red Sox fan. However, I did my best to fairly negotiate with the Red Sox and Yankees, aka, the Evil Empire! During this time, it really was enjoyable to meet the management team of both clubs. The highlight of this was when I was in Boston for a conference and visited the Red Sox and received a personal tour of Fenway Park, including walking out on the field with the team's general manager. At the time I did not realize that I would later be even more engaged with the Red Sox.

At the beginning of my tenure with the city, the mayor and council told me that they wanted me to meet with the Atlanta organization and negotiate a deal for them to stay in Greenville and to build a new stadium near Downtown Greenville. The city and the Braves had been in negotiation for this to happen for more than four years and the team had more than once said they would move to another market if a deal, acceptable to them, could not be reached. The city council told me they were willing to spend all of three million dollars to support this effort, more than a little shy of what was needed.

I immediately started a dialog with the Braves general management, led by Mike Plant, the operations vice president. Mike and I became friends through this process. Mike was an outstanding Olympic speed skater. He would have likely been a household name had he not competed at the same time as one of his friends in their native Wisconsin named Eric Heiden. From 2013 to 2108 Mike served as the President of US

164

Speedskating. At the time I remember being anxious to see how his children took to sports since he married Mary T. Meagher, aka, Madam Butterfly. For those who do not follow swimming Mary held the world record in the 100 and 200 Butterfly for more 19 and 20 years respectively. Those two record swims are ranked as some of the greatest sports feats ever. Later in my tenure as the Greenville City Manager, I would cross paths with Mike in the world of bike racing. This will be described later in this chapter.

From the very beginning of our discussions, it was clear that the Braves expected the city to build a new stadium entirely at the city's cost. Furthermore, the Braves were weary of negotiating with the city and publicly gave the city a few weeks to culminate a deal or they would move the team to Mississippi. We negotiated over what revenues the city could retain from the operation such as ticket sales, stadium suite purchases, concessions and player development fees, normally paid to the minor league team operator. The cost of a minor league stadium was placed at from $24 to $25 million based on the recent Atlanta experience in Rome, Georgia. In Rome, the city had indeed built a stadium for the Braves A level team.

Regardless of the revenue package that the Braves might agree to allow the city to retain, we were a long way away from what the city council would be willing to pay. The deal would have likely cost the city $24 million, a good $21 million more than the council had originally been willing to shell out.

In a final negotiation in Atlanta one evening over dinner, Mike Plant and I amicably agreed that we were not going to be able to reach mutually agreeable terms. We agreed to make a joint announcement that we could not reach an acceptable arrangement. I need to hasten to add that all along the way, the city council was continually briefed and they were in agreement with this move. When the announcement came, many in the city were most disappointed. The Braves had been a fixture in the city for decades and there were many fans of the major league team, located only a couple of hours down the road. I certainly took a significant amount of heat for recommending that the city walk away from completing a deal. Many citizens would have gladly supported the city spending the money to build a stadium for the team.

However, I felt, along with city council backing, that it was not in the interest of the city to spend around $24 million dollars to retain the team. This was partially due to my belief from conversation with people knowledgeable of Minor League Baseball, that the Greenville market would be very attractive for a Minor League ownership group, which proved to be absolutely true.

At the same time as announcing the end of negotiation with the Braves, we announced that we were seeking another minor league team to locate in the city. If I felt the heat when coming to town and being tasked with getting an agreement with Atlanta, there was even more pressure to recruit a team and get a deal done to keep Minor League Baseball in Greenville. The city has a long and noteworthy history with baseball which includes the boyhood home of Shoeless Joe Jackson.

I will spare the reader all the intricacies of minor league baseball and everything we went through before signing an agreement. To summarize, I talked to many ownership groups and potential ownership groups. We had serious proposals from five groups vying to put a team in Greenville. One of the most serious proposals was from Mandalay Entertainment. They already had a number of very successful minor league franchises operating in the US. However, they wanted a very elaborate stadium with a sophisticated jumbotron score board and the price tag was well north of 30 million. Remember, this was in 2004 when the costs were a lot less than they are today.   When talking to my lead contact with Mandalay, I remember saying that their proposal was significantly more expensive than it needed to be and much more than we could afford.

The best offer was from a group which included three principal owners who were interested in moving their team from Columbia, South Carolina to Greenville. This was only after they had expended great effort to come to terms with the City of Columbia on a new stadium. The situation there was significantly complicated by the desire for a joint facility for the city and the University of South Carolina. This ownership group proposed a deal that they would build the stadium while retaining the basic revenue streams from its operation. They believed and it was undoubtedly true that they could construct the stadium for a lower cost than the city could. We would provide a site and the infrastructure to the site. On a personal note, their player development agreement was, at the time, with the New York Mets. However, they were getting ready to enter into a new agreement with another franchise. They had a strong connection with, coincidently, the Boston Red Sox. That really had nothing to do with my recommendation to go with them, REALLY! It was the best arrangement by far and the best deal for any city with a Minor League team around that time.

This was a match made in heaven from my perspective. The team agreed to play the next season in the old city stadium while we worked with them on building a new field in the Downtown Greenville area. We picked a site and I negotiated for the land acquisition. That was particularly tricky since the city council publicly said they would not use their condemnation powers. This was because of a very difficult experience with a redevelopment project where they had condemned property prior to the 2005 Kelo v. City of New London US Supreme Court Decision that put a very negative spin on the use of eminent domain. The Greenville County court decision on the amount the city had to pay came after the Kelo ruling. The City ended up spending more than double the amount to acquire the land than the appraised amount.

Nevertheless, we acquired the 7.5 acre site and worked with the team on a joint development which included the stadium and a four story mixed-use building including ground level retail, office and condominiums adjacent to the field. With a player development agreement signed with the Red Sox, the field was designed as an exact replica of Fenway Park in Boston, including a Green Monster wall in the outfield. There is wide agreement that it is an awesome field. It won the award for the best new baseball stadium the year it opened. This award encompassed all baseball stadiums, including Major League stadiums, like the St. Louis Cardinals Busch Stadium which also opened that year. Additionally, it was received very well by Boston with at least two major articles in the Boston Globe about the field.

I must say a word about the construction process. We had a most aggressive schedule of only 10 months from acquiring the land ownership to opening day. This included relocating just about all utilities known to man which traversed the site, including water, sewer, stormwater, gas, telephone and electric lines. We had an amazing level of cooperation among the team ownership group, the architects, the construction firm, the developers of the mixed use building and the city staff. Although we were laying down the final layer of asphalt on an adjacent street the morning of opening day, we got it done on time.

In addition, the bottom line for the city was a financial success. The city spent $10 million to acquire the property, run utilities to the site and provide streetscaping from the edge of the main part of downtown to the site, a bit more than a quarter of a mile. This represented a savings of about $14 million over what it would have cost to accommodate the Atlanta Braves and many more times than that to ink a deal with Mandalay. I was particularly gratified when the Mandalay representative came to Greenville to look at the stadium and made a point of contacting me to say that I was right, it did not need to cost as much as they had proposed.

It also needs to be mentioned that the team that ultimately came to Greenville was not a Double A team like the city had been accustomed to for so many years but a lower level Single A team. I did catch some flak from some big baseball enthusiasts. However, most people coming to see Minor League Baseball really cannot distinguish between a step down in the level. In fact, the year the stadium opened it broke the all-time attendance mark set by the AA Atlanta Braves. And they broke that again the following year and then again the next year.

Another significant footnote to this story is that the Braves did indeed move their AA Team to Mississippi. While they may have felt it was a good financial move since they signed a favorable deal, it appeared to be a bit penny wise but pound foolish. For the first couple of years, the Greenville A team outdrew the Mississippi Braves AA Team by an average of over 2,000 fans per game.

Baseball stadium, named Fluor Field Under construction

The field and stadium have become a fixture in the community and have contributed greatly to the revitalization of the downtown and surrounding area. This will be described further in a later chapter. With not only baseball but other community events held at the venue, I refer to the field as the city's "living room". Cities have greatly benefited from sports teams; sometimes spending wisely and sometimes paying a ransom. I know all too well that saying no is not easy and always wish the best to any city running that gambit. I attended dozens of games in the stadium and every time felt great exhilaration in being in the stadium and knowing I played a part in making the experience possible. Watching the fans enjoy themselves was indeed a big reward.

Big Crowd at the baseball stadium for the team known as the Greenville Drive

In addition, who you do business with is quite important. The three principal owners were upstanding business executives that got into baseball because they really wanted to be engaged in the sport. It was not to make a lot of money, they had already done that. One of the owners, Craig Brown, had played a more active role and ended up buying the interest of his two partners in the team. Craig and his wife, Vicki, have moved to Greenville and Craig has become a community leader in their newly adopted hometown. He is a pure class act and has become a good friend.

Shoeless Joe Jackson takes the field at the opening game in 2006 (that is , an actor playing him)

USA Pro Cycling Championships

Baseball was not the only sport that my position in Greenville involved me in which a public private partnership was critical to its success for the city. Prior to my time in Greenville, the City had been engaged in cycling events. Through these events, the city was known to a company called Medalist Sports. This company had been started by Mike Plant who had not only been an excellent speed skater but also an accomplished cyclist after he concluded his competitive speed skating career. After I arrived in the city, through conversation with people from Medalist Sports, we learned of a potential opportunity to host the USA Pro Cycling Championships. These races consisted of the time trial championships (an event where cyclists ride as individuals with a staggered start, along a closed course, shorter than the road race, and the winner is based on the fastest time) as well as the road race (a relatively long race, generally exceeding 100 miles on a relatively hilly course).

These championship events had been staged in Philadelphia for more than 20 years, the entire time of their existence. However, there was an opportunity to move to another city. This would require a commitment from the city to host the event as well as a concerted effort to raise funds to support racing operations. I immediately went to the council to get their support, which they enthusiastically provided. We worked with Medalist Sports on a proposal and were successful in luring the championships to Greenville. This necessitated raising approximately $500,000 annually from private sources. I realize that not all managers may feel comfortable with this role but I was fine in leading this effort. Without the existing contacts I had built up with business leaders we would not have been able to raise the funding.

For seven years Greenville hosted the USA Cycling Championships and gained a tremendous amount of worldwide recognition. It has always been hard for people to wrap their mind around the over 100 million media exposures we received each year! The race was opened for proposals from Greenville and other cities after I left my position as the manager. The city staff told me they did not submit a bid because no one with the city could have raised the funding needed. It was a good seven year run and had broad benefits. As I was departing the city, one of the US racing stars who was from Greenville and had won two national championships, George Hincapie, presented me with one of his USA Cycling Championship jerseys for the role I played in bringing the National Championships to Greenville. That was very special to me.

The event also assisted in our economic development effort. One never really knows the benefits that some efforts will produce. Early on in the years Greenville hosted the event, we learned of a group of Canadian cyclists who had done a CEO cycling experience in the area arranged by a group that promotes sporting experiences for those that can afford this sort of activity. We offered to host this group in Greenville for the Cycling Championships. They took us up on the invitation and we formed some important relationships with a few of the CEOs. One of the individuals was the head of the Canadian operation of TD Bank. The bank had been expanding into US markets. While in Greenville, they were introduced to executives with Carolina First Bank which was really struggling within the current banking environment at that time.

Carolina First, a regional bank with its corporate headquarters in Greenville, was a major corporate entity. Later in this chapter, I will describe one of the projects they had supported. If Carolina First had gone under, it would have been a huge loss for the city. However, just prior to the bank failing, TD Bank purchased it. TD Bank executives were familiar with the bank and their leaders through the trip to Greenville. Not only did the city retain the business activity of Carolina First, but TD Bank established a regional operations center in Greenville with hundreds of additional jobs initially and many more to come. The cycling championships and hosting the group of Canadians had paid a huge dividend.

The crowd at the USA Pro Cycling Championships

Research parks

Greenville has many excellent examples of public-private partnerships that have greatly enhanced the city. Another major effort I was involved with was development of the Clemson International Center for Automotive Research (ICAR). This is a 250-acre research and office campus developed on land that was owned by a past wealthy industrialist, JD Hollingsworth. He believed in acquiring and holding on to land as a great asset. He had acquired large tracks in and near the city as well as further away. When he died, he designated charities that would

174

reap the return from the land sales. In addition to this portion of land, there was another 11,000-acre track on the other side of Interstate 85 that was developed into a tremendous city asset. This will also be described.

The ICAR development brought high tech research operations and additional higher education into the city. Clemson University, with its main campus about 30 miles away from Greenville, saw an opportunity to take advantage of the more urban area of Greenville to attract high quality students and team with companies doing advanced research and manufacturing in the automotive industry. This industry had been well represented for many years in the Greenville area with the North American headquarters of Michelin and a large BMW automobile assembly facility. Both Michelin and BMW were participants in ICAR. Other technology and auto related businesses joined the effort. The city provided the external and internal infrastructure to assist the development of this tremendous economic asset for the area.

The investment in this project also helped to fuel the development of another adjacent research/office park with such major investments as the new headquarters for Hubbell Lighting and the regional headquarters of TD Bank. These and other companies brought thousands of jobs to the City of Greenville. The key ingredients for this success were the large tract of available land, the public investment in necessary infrastructure and the catalyst of the Clemson Graduate School of Automotive Engineering in partnership with key private industries in that sector.

I was also involved in a similar Research/Office development in Newport News. This had many of the same elements. Newport News is home to Jefferson National Laboratories, a facility established for atomic particle research. This institution receives funding from the US Department of Energy and operates a particle accelerator which smashes atoms to study their makeup. The laboratory was eyeing the expansion of their efforts with an electron ion collider. While not getting into the physics of this, it is important to note that the capital investment would

175

likely be around a billion dollars for the expansion and contribute an estimated $4 billion to the area's economy and create 4,000 new jobs. Whether or not the expansion would happen, the City of Newport News was very interested in taking advantage of technology that might come out of the research at Jefferson Laboratory. In addition, there was available land for development adjacent to this facility.

Much of the credit for this development, which is still evolving, needs to go to a community leader, John Lawson, who was the president and lead owner of a construction and land development firm, WM Jordan. He understood the vision of creating a mixed-use development including retail, residential and office/research space. He acquired a key piece of property and jump started the development with retail and residential uses. The controversial rezoning for this development was done during the first month of my tenure with the city. As in Greenville, I had to jump in with two feet, legs, arms, etc. and get immersed up to my neck in the project very quickly. Of course, I knew a lot about it because of my background research prior to interviewing. Realizing its critical importance to framing the future of the city, I advocated for the project with the city council. My first council meeting went up to midnight with the approval of this project. Normally council meetings generally ran from 7:00 PM to about 8:00 PM.

The development of the research office park has followed a pattern very familiar to me. In addition to Jefferson National Lab and WM Jordan, the partners in the project included Virginia Tech University and the city. The city is providing the infrastructure, WM Jordan is developing the property and the University is leading the push for developing intellectual property. To me this is a winning formula. The plan is to build one million square feet of office/research space. Aside from helping to sheppard this project forward, one of my biggest contributions to this project was to push the square footage from an envisioned 500,000 to one million. While

Newport News has been the home of great manufacturing companies, this project is critical for driving the city into higher technology businesses.

New town, In town

Let's get back to the additional Hollingsworth 1,100-acre tract of land in Greenville which was used for another hugely important development. This development has become what urban planners refer to as a "New Town, In Town". That is, an entirely new, almost self-sustaining development of such scale and magnitude that it could virtually stand by itself as a town or city. Plans envision, when complete, a community of 10,000 residents, 550 businesses and 15,000 jobs, with an estimated investment of 2.2 billion dollars. This is huge for a city with the physical size and population of Greenville. As a new development, it offers the opportunity to provide new lifestyle options in a developed city. The community is based on neotraditional community design which helps to create a strong community as well as reduce the need for commuting with its mixture of living, shopping and employment.

Public private redevelopment

While an entire chapter is devoted to the revitalization of downtowns, this chapter includes some redevelopment outside of downtown. In the City of Newport News, there is a key redevelopment project in an older area with lower income residents, significant crime and deteriorating structures. The project is called Brooks Crossing, reflecting the engagement of Aaron Brooks, a well-known professional football player from Newport News. A private developer had partnered with the city for a commercial project that was intended to be an impetus for a turnaround for this district. However, the project had languished, in part due to the economic downturn late in the first decade of the 2000s and, in part, because of a lack of confidence of potential private investors.

The project was designed to include a badly needed grocery store as the area was in a classic food dessert. The last grocery store left shortly after my arrival to the city. Also planned was a police precinct to not only provide coverage for the southern part of town, but also to serve as a partial response to the high crime rate.

So, here we go again; Bourey enters stage right and is immediately faced with another critically important project that had languished for years. Of course, I have never been one to shy away from a challenge or push the envelope, which was certainly necessary for this project. Prior to my arrival, the city had been reluctant to move forward with the police precinct until the private sector committed to significant development. However, I felt that one of the parties needed to make a commitment to get the development moving forward. Fortunately, we had pushed an upgrade in the city's credit rating with a trip to New York to Moody's and Standard and Poor's where we successfully gained an upgrade to the city's credit rating. This not only saved millions for the city in the next bond issue but also generated six million dollars in extra funding.

I proposed, and the city council agreed to the concept of using this money to fund most of the police precinct costs and get the development moving. This indeed provided a boost to the project. However, the lack of a grocery store in the area remained a major community concern. The city staff had previously talked to any grocery chain that might have been remotely interested in building a store, with no success. We undertook another round of inquiries with the commitment to build the police precinct, with no takers.

This is another instance where I took a step with which other managers would not necessarily feel comfortable. Please remember I am not saying how I have done business is the way and only way it should be done; every manager must choose their own path. I proposed to the city council that the city build a store and lease it to a private operator. The lease payments could help to retire the debt for the capital cost. In addition, I proposed pursuing New Market Tax Credits to assist with the capital cost. While not getting into the intricacies of how these tax credits work, they are a vehicle that could be used to write down the cost of the capital construction by about 20%. They are **very** complicated, and I sometimes refer to them as welfare for attorneys. I had been quite familiar with their use in projects for Downtown Greenville. While this was an aggressive step for the City, it was clear and is still obvious that it was the only way to get a full-service grocery store in the community.

There was great fanfare and excitement when it opened. The operator the city picked was a long time grocery executive who had left the grocery chain business to give back to communities by providing stores in food deserts. Unfortunately, even as involved as he became with the community, he was viewed as an outsider and the store suffered from a high level of shoplifting. Sadly, the people in the community who he gave jobs to largely looked the other way as their friends stole from the store. The original operator has given way to a successful second operator and the store is a great asset to the community.

With some good momentum for the development, we negotiated with Newport News Shipbuilding to build a major office and research building on the site, bringing hundreds of people to the area. These are the types of projects that can reinforce the feeling that you are making a difference for people and a community. They do outweigh the less pleasant aspects of the job.

Privately operated public facilities

I have previously described the renovation of the Carolina First Center in Greenville, which was also a public private partnership effort in its own right. I would like to highlight the private operation of this facility as another successful partnership. Although having a private operator of a publicly owned convention center is very common, this is highlighted because the operation of facilities like convention centers and arenas can make some of the best partnerships. This has worked so well, in part, because there is a sharing or revenues of the profitability beyond set levels. This gives the operator an incentive to be productive but keeps the city with a stake in the game.

The renovation of the facility provided the opportunity to expand the capacity for a sit down dinner approaching 2,000 people. It was always amazing how the dining service could deliver warm and excellent meals to a banquet of well over 1,500 people with timely service to hundreds of tables.

This chapter has provided many examples of public-private partnership projects. I would suggest that these projects help to illustrate certain lessons for these partnerships, including the following:

- Be willing to walk away from a deal that is not in the best interest of the community

- Know the market and the community's desirability whether it is for a Minor League baseball team or a research park

- Weigh the benefits vs the cost to the city/county, but be sure to look at benefits broadly such as the wide ranging publicity of the US Pro Cycling Championships and a Minor League Baseball stadium that hosts many other events

- Work the public private partnership to ensure that both sides reap benefits in the deal

- Add a mixed use development to assist in the viability of single purpose projects

- Take advantage of a community's assets such as a world class federal research lab

- Be willing to play a vital role in raising private donations to support a project

- Understand the critical roles of providing public infrastructure for private projects

- Partnering with universities and colleges can add a vital dimension for a development

- Having the city/county take the lead in projects where that initiative is vital in moving a development forward

- Sometimes only the public sector can build a facility and other times the private sector can build it more cost effectively

- In some instances the private sector can operate a facility more effectively than the public

Often in doing public-private partnerships, the city or county is asked to take on a certain amount of risk. Evaluating whether that risk is acceptable or not is most critical. The next chapter explores that issue.

Chapter Thirteen

Big Risk, Big reward; How Much Risk is Appropriate

In the last chapter, the reasonably big risk the city took to build a grocery store was described. There was certainly a great reward with the success of the store. And I believe the risk was well worth it. But how much risk is appropriate and prudent for a public entity to take is an important question.   Local government managers are charged with protecting the public interest but getting things done is also in the public interest.   Sometimes things do not get done without taking some measured risk. The question is what a reasonable risk for a governmental entity to take? I will describe a situation where many second guessed the level of risk and most observers felt the risk was too great.

People Express, an ugly chapter

This is not an easy story for me to tell, because I have questioned my actions since the venture I voted in favor of as a Newport News-Williamsburg Airport Authority Board member went south. As a fallout from this failed project not only did I resign my position on the airport authority but also as City Manager for Newport News and as a result stepped down from positions as the Chairman of the Hampton Roads Economic Development Association and the Chair of the Hampton Roads City and County Managers Group as well as on the board of the local chamber of commerce. I also was asked to step aside as the Chairman of the Peninsula United Way Campaign for the year. None of this was because I had done anything wrong but did support a funding strategy in which public funds were at risk, and it did not work. While my vote was conceptually independent of my city manager position, the negative public sentiment raised by the newspaper's sensationalistic journalism pushed the council into forcing my resignation.

Hindsight is always 20-20 and if I had to do it all again, I would certainly not support the effort. I really believe the purported upside of the deal led the board to go forward and perhaps clouded the wisdom of supporting it. While you can judge whether or not you would have voted to proceed, we cannot take away the fact that we know how it all turned out. But then, I am way ahead of myself in the narrative. While this story is extremely complex, I will attempt to summarize, make it as readable as possible, and not bore you with all the complexities that are unnecessary to tell the story.

Newport News is served by the Newport News-Williamsburg International Airport (NNWA), although some people end up using either the Norfolk or Richmond Airports to seek other flight options. Upon my arrival in the city, the airport was suffering from the loss of much of the airport flight capacity due to the buyout of AirTran by Southwest Airlines and the move of all their extensive flights from NNWA to Norfolk where Southwest operated. In this one change the airport lost 40% of its flights and key non-stop destinations such as New York City. The Airport was aggressively trying to replace this service when I started with the city. This was viewed as essential to city economic development efforts.

The NNWA is governed by a Board consisting of four appointees of the Newport News City Council and two appointed by the City of Hampton. A long time city manager who had served while the manager as well as after he retired, relocated from the City just after my arrival. With his departure the city council appointed me to serve on the NNWA Board. The city council and the board were all in agreement that replacing the lost air service at the airport was a very high priority.

In order to support the airport recruitment of airline service, many cities in the local area had formed a support group and had dedicated funding to attract air service. This funding had been used over the past few years to provide a subsidy to airlines for committing to provide service at the airport. Prior to my arrival funds of more than $700,000 had been committed by this group for use as a match for a Small Airport Assistance Grant, a US grant program that helps airports expand service.

Also prior to me joining the city, the airport had been working with a potential start-up airline that was envisioned as a reincarnation of People Express, which was a low cost airline that had effectively served the East Coast. The proposed service would largely replace the passenger capacity lost when Southwest Airlines cannibalized the service. After Southwest Airlines had moved the service to Norfolk, they eliminated most of the Norfolk service over time. It was quite apparent that the move to buy Air Tran was a move to eliminate a rival, especially with their direct competitive service out of Atlanta. This new NNWA service would include non-stop service to New York and would have been a homerun for the area.

A former employee of People Express was leading this effort. This new People Express airline had obtained some funding, including over one million dollars from local businessmen. However, although they had received some substantial commitments from sources totaling over five million, they were struggling to get the capital to launch the effort. Venture capital funds to support new airline startups is very difficult to come by.

The challenge in raising funding was despite a very robust business plan that showed an excellent opportunity to quickly build ridership for the airline which was to be based at NNWA. This plan of operations and revenue generation was reviewed and endorsed by the NNWA Executive Director, who believed it was very likely to be successful. After many more months of the airline's unsuccessful attempts to get the funding, the airport director came up with a plan to jump start the service. His plan was to have the airport guarantee a five million dollar loan for start-up funding for the airline.

His plan was for the guarantee of funds to be provided from three sources, the Federal Small Airport Assistance Grant, the funding from the cities which had been previously pledged as a match for the grant and state funds flowing to the airport. The director and the attorney for the board both vouched for the legality and appropriateness of the proposal. In addition, other attorneys looking at the transaction saw no issues with the terms of the agreement.

The proforma for the airline showed a relatively quick return of revenue that would be able to pay off the loan. Moreover, the airline had hired as their CEO the former head of TWA; someone who had successfully led a west coast startup similar to the planned People Express initiative. A loan was obtained from a local bank and the airline was launched with great community enthusiasm and excellent initial bookings.

As indicated, I will keep this as straightforward as possible, but some complexity is necessary to tell the tale. For airlines to operate, they must have an operations certification which includes voluminous documentation. Many airlines, especially startups, contract with existing airlines for their initial operation. Indeed, many large airlines contract with smaller regional carriers to provide service for shorter trips in their network. Each of the major carriers does this. For instance, last year United Airlines had eight airline partners in its network.

People Express contracted with Vision Air to provide the initial air service. That ended up being one of the weak links in the chain of events that ultimately led to an unravelling of the service. Vision Air never provided the full number of planes and crews which were part of their agreement. Vision claimed they did not get the payments that were required in their agreement. This led to difficulties in delivering service when any mechanical issue came up. It would have likely worked if the full range of support had been provided. Whether People Express or Vision was at fault, I will not draw a conclusion. This situation came to a head when a worker servicing one of the planes in Newport News, who was not authorized to operate the equipment, ran into one of the planes, opening a hole in it and putting it out of commission. It seems that the startup was star crossed. By the projections, it should have been successful but, it was not.

While there was certainly some potential recourse for People Express to recover some damages, nothing could really happen in a timely enough fashion to get the airline back to being operational. There were other operators and potential sources of funding that might have worked but no deal was consummated. Due to the lack of revenue, the loan to the airline had to be repaid by the airport as pledged.

The community was disappointed that the airline ceased operations, but things did not hit the fan at that point because the newspaper reporter covering the airport frequently did not always attend the airport authority meetings at that time. This was, in part, because they started at 8:00 AM and we know reporters do not like to get up early. In addition, the newspaper had not reviewed the annual audit that showed the repayment of the loan. The paper ultimately picked up on the loan repayment when a disgruntled airport vendor notified a reporter.

It was certainly apparent that the paper was embarrassed that they totally missed the agreement for the loan and the repayment. However, they were also unhappy with the city and the city manager, in particular. They had previously assigned a rookie reporter to cover the city and she was very inaccurate in her writing. The city had to repeatedly inform the paper of errors. The reporter suddenly left the paper to no surprise of anyone with the city. However, the editor held a grudge against the city and its manager which helped the situation play out over the next year.

Another dimension needs to be added to the story. The governor at the time, who attended the People Express announcement, had suffered a significant recent embarrassment when an economic development deal went south. The state had paid a large incentive for a Chinese company to locate a manufacturing operation in an economically depressed part of Virginia. The company had kept the money and did not deliver the proposed facility and jobs. When the governor heard of the use of state money to repay the People Express loan, he instructed the head of the state department of transportation to aggressively react to the loan guarantee and repayment. This gave the paper plenty of ammunition to attack the deal.

The actual state money used amounted to $3.5 million. I do not want, in any way, to diminish this amount but need to put the situation in context. The head of the transportation department had recently been involved in two major state transactions. While on the state transportation board he had voted to approve a public private partnership for a major state road extension that ran into difficulties. The State ended up paying out more than $260 million to the private party and getting basically nothing in return. Also, when on the state transportation board, he had supported a public-private partnership agreement for expanded tunnel access to downtown Norfolk that was to be paid for with toll revenues. The agreement provided that if the state built another water crossing into the city or an expansion of capacity of an existing one, the state would owe the private entity a payment to replace their potential loss of revenue, despite that it is questionable whether the new crossing would even decrease the private sector entity's revenue. While it is not yet known, this payment was estimated in a *Washington Post* article to be in the range of between $269 and $774 million over the life of the agreement. Folks, those are pretty big bucks and represent a major financial impact.

Again, $3.5 million is significant. However, the huge state money loss on these deals were reported only in passing by the paper. On the other hand the airport loss was chronicled day after day after day. In a year the paper ran more than 200 articles, mostly on the front page above the fold, each time with little or virtually no new information.

Remember when I said that it is best not to get on the bad side of a paper? We all know the adage that papers buy ink in bulk! It was brutal! Even though my role was as a voting member of the six member airport board, I was the highest profile member and had led many initiatives. This made me an easy target for the paper. The airport executive director also caught a lot of flak. Sometime later, we found out that the director had done things behind the scenes, unknown to the board, that were problematic.

Was it a reasonable risk to take to guarantee the loan? Would I do it again? The answer to the second question is an obvious **hell no,** in hindsight. The answer to the first is a bit more complicated. However, I think that the board (me included) was too caught up in the pot of gold at the end of this airport service rainbow and should not have approved the loan guarantee. While it was not illegal or unethical, it was simply too much of a risk. The support for the agreement and my vote will haunt me for the rest of my life. As well intentioned as it was, I surely do regret it.

This is the only time I recall where taking a significant risk came back to haunt me. In negotiating deals, I always say, we have got to be willing to walk away or we may end up holding the short end of the stick. Boy how, I wish we would have walked away!

As a footnote to this story, it turns out that some of the actions that the executive director took behind the scenes that the board members were not aware of were judged to be illegal. These included manipulation of some of the funding used for repayment of the loan as well as other transactions that ran him afoul of federal regulations. He was prosecuted for those transgressions and I served as a Federal witness, largely to testify what the board did not know. Additionally, the lead person in the People Express resurrection had committed some fund manipulation and tax fraud.

In sitting as an Airport Authority Board member, I relied heavily on the executive director, just as managers expect their councils to rely on them. If I had to do it all over again, I would push the board to do more due diligence and rely less on the executive director. As I said, an **ugly chapter**!

Seattle Good Neighbor Program

Now we can shift to a story that once again involved a measure of risk but does have a happier ending! This occurred during the time I was the Director of the Office for Planning with the City of Seattle. Many years earlier, the city had owned and operated a landfill in the nearby City of Kent. The landfill had been closed and was subject to closure activities. This included a methane gas burn off system. However, the city discovered that the methane gas was migrating from the landfill under a strata of rock to a 1,000 home subdivision. It was so significant that potentially explosive levels were found in some basements and those homes needed to be evacuated. Multiple claims had been filed against the city.

The city was quite confident that the methane could be controlled but that would take some time and the neighborhood, quite naturally, was concerned with not only their safety but the value of their homes. In fact, the neighbors were organizing to file a class action lawsuit against the city. My department became involved to deal with the neighborhood issues.

We developed an action plan we called the Good Neighbor Program. The program provided a guarantee that the city would buy any home in the area that people wanted to sell at the market rate prior to the discovery of the methane gas. Further, the city would buy it at that time or later if they wanted to sell, again at the market rate without the presence of the gas.

The idea was to head off the class action suit and any panic selling. We were quite confident that any home the city purchased could be resold at market value after the methane gas was controlled. Due to the city's guarantee of purchase and that their property values would be maintained, very few took us up on the offer to purchase. The city was able to effectively resell those homes after fixing the methane gas problem. The Good Neighbor Program cost very little at the conclusion and saved the city potentially millions that it would have had to pay out in a class action suit.

While there was a measure of risk involved in instituting the program, the potential downside would likely still have been better than a class action lawsuit and the upside was tremendous. Additionally, there was not a significant likelihood that a large number of homeowners would have wanted to sell their homes as it was a stable and nice neighborhood that people enjoyed. So, the risk then and in hindsight seems appropriate.

Hillsborough County sludge handling facility

We took another calculated risk with a project that had a terrific outcome when I was with Hillsborough County. You know from a previous chapter, that I led the development and execution of a very large water and wastewater construction program. The design and construction of these facilities occurred in the late 1980s and early 1990s. During most of this time, the federal program which provided grants for the some of the construction cost for wastewater facilities was still available. While the initial grant match the federal program provided had been well in excess of a 50% match, the program was reduced to half the project cost by this time. In addition, the grant program was being phased out in favor of providing loans.

The grant program was winding down when the county was ready to provide a sludge handling facility for solids coming out of the regional sewerage treatment plants being completed. We were in a position to be able to get grant funding only for a relatively short time when this project was getting underway. In order to qualify for a grant, we needed an approved design for the construction of the facility. The time for design and approval process for this $40 million project would generally have been close to a year and certainly well over six months. We had approximately three months to get an approved design and qualify for a $20 million grant. Most felt that this was not doable. However, I really wanted to give it a chance. I asked staff to develop a contract with the engineering firm that gave them a 10% bonus to their fee if they produced a design that was approved in time for us to obtain the grant. We also included a 10% penalty if they were not successful in getting the design done in time. Thus, the real incentive to the engineering firm was a 20% swing in their fee. They would either make a good bit of money or maybe just clear their costs.

The firm was successful in producing a design that was approved and the county received a grant in excess of $20 million. The engineering firm was well paid for their effort and the county had a windfall. In this case, the risk to the county was relatively minimal. We needed the design and would have had to pay for it anyway. If we were not successful in obtaining the grant, the design would have cost us less than market rate. Since we were successful, the economic benefit dwarfed the higher design fee.

In looking at the examples described, it seems to me one of the takeaways is to fully recognize what the worst outcome of taking the risk would be. In the case of building the grocery store, the city would always have the asset of the building whether or not it was successful and be able to go to another operator, which it ultimately did do. In the case of the Good Neighbor Program, the city would have the asset of the homes to resell. In the case of People Express, the downside of the failure of the airline left the airport authority with almost no residual benefit. Looking at it from that perspective gives a good lens to evaluate a decision.

So what are the takeaways from these examples:

- Examine the upside as well as the downside of any proposal and whether the benefit outweighs the risk

- Find ways to backstop the level of risk, the grocery store was still going to be an asset as were the houses that the city might have had to buy

- If the downside is just not an acceptable outcome, then the risk is not worth taking

- Do your own due diligence and the higher the stakes, the more due diligence is necessary

- Trust but verify; it is fine to have confidence in the people that bring you proposals but there are other avenues to validate proposals

- Don't get on the bad side of the media

- Recognize there may be repercussions if you are not successful

We have examined public-private partnerships and local governments evaluating the level of risk that they might take. These and many other issues are present in the efforts of communities to re-invigorate their downtowns. We will now move on to look at successful downtown development.

Chapter Fourteen

Successful Downtown Development

Many books have been written on the topic of downtown revitalization and offer great insight into how to go about such efforts. As in past chapters, I will not duplicate those valuable resources. Rather, this will once again describe the approaches to downtown revitalization that I have found to be especially helpful. In doing this, I will rely heavily on my experience with the downtown development efforts while the Greenville City Manager.

I need to first provide a bit of context for Greenville, as many readers will not be familiar with this area. Greenville is located in what is referred to as *Upstate South Carolina.* It is in the northeastern part of the state along I-85 between Charlotte and Atlanta. It is only about 90 minutes from Charlotte and about two hours (the way I drive) from Atlanta. Greenville has remained a relatively small city geographically over time due to the very stringent annexation laws in the state, while the county has grown to well over 500,000 people. If Greenville had been in North Carolina with the annexation laws that existed at the time of its major growth, I suspect the population would be well over 300,000 or 400,000 instead of roughly 70,000. Despite the constrained boundaries and population, Greenville has a very large daytime population due to the employment base. It is hard to pinpoint an exact number, but the daytime population easily exceeds 150,000.

Certainly, the efforts to revitalize Downtown Greenville began long before I arrived. The downtown was once a very vibrant place with substantial retail, especially along Main Street, the major roadway through downtown. However, like so many downtowns across the country, much of the retail had moved out to shopping malls. The downtown was left with a four-lane thoroughfare that went through it.

The city made a concerted effort to improve this situation and invested in streetscape improvements, including street trees along Main Street. The street trees, in particular, were met with skepticism by the local newspaper, the *Greenville News,* who editorialized that "no amount of money will ever save downtown." Fortunately, the rejuvenation of Downtown Greenville proved them wrong, although it did take decades to realize that success. I need to take a moment to give a bit of a shout out to the Greenville News. While the newspaper aspires to get things openly and accurately reported, they do not believe that means to always be negative and tear down what people are trying to accomplish. While being fair and objective, the paper has generally acted in the best interest of the community.

The city did not gain much traction on redevelopment until a Hyatt Regency was built along Main Street in the 1980s, aided by an Urban Development Action Grant, a federal funding program at that time. Still progressing rather slowly, the downtown and Main Street got another significant boost in 1990 with the construction of the Peace Center for the Performing Arts, built several blocks south of the Hyatt. This world class center with two theaters helped to bring more people back to downtown. However, Main Street was still perceived as an unsafe place by many citizens. At the same time, the turnaround had gained some momentum and progress was being made.

Peace Center for the Performing Arts 1

In 2004 when I became the City Manager, things were starting to look up for downtown and it was moving forward. However, a number of projects completed in the rest of the decade brought the incredible success that has been studied by so many other cities. Certainly right at the top of the list of these projects was Falls Park. Hopefully many of the readers have been to Greenville and have seen Falls Park and that many will go if you have not seen the park and downtown.

While virtually no downtown has a major 40 foot waterfall in the heart of downtown, it took years of effort and inspired leadership to translate this natural feature into an amazing asset.

Reedy River Falls in Downtown Greenville

For decades the waterfall, fed by the Reedy River, was virtually covered over by a four-lane state roadway. Several people, including Mayor Knox White (who is still Mayor), basically developed a campaign to "free the falls." Despite the warnings of many that eliminating this roadway link would lead to significant traffic problems, the bridge was removed. This allowed the development of an amazing 32-acre park, highlighted by a 355 foot long 12 foot wide suspension bridge over the falls. This park was opened about nine months after my arrival and helped to solidify the unique downtown experience.

The extremely popular foot bridge over the falls1

One of the next two major boosts for downtown was the first phase of the mixed use, 720,000 square foot RiverPlace development, slightly upstream from the falls. Including office, retail, a hotel, residences and a city parking garage, this project contributed another level of activity and interest in the downtown. Subsequent phases have added a great deal more to this landmark project. The second and very transformational project was Fluor Field, the Minor League Baseball stadium previously described. This extended redevelopment of Main Street about a half a

River Place development

mile further south and has led to the revitalization of a large area which continues to astound observers.

There were many additional projects that followed like the redo of the area around City Hall, another project I put a lot of personal energy into. This project, Main at Broad, consisted of a hotel, destination restaurant, retail, office and parking garage as well as a great green square. The redevelopment of downtown Greenville achieved an incredible

Open courtyard at the Main at Broad project

momentum that has only accelerated and continues to amaze locals and delight visitors. Ok, you get it, I am very partial to the downtown!

So, what are some of the things that helped to build its success? Are there principles that can be transferred to other settings? I would like to offer the following suggestions for other downtowns:

A strong public private partnership
As has been stressed before, a successful public-private partnership drives development and progress. Those relationships must be built on a foundation of

trust among the parties. Furthermore, there must be consistency in the public sector services and rules and regulations as well as public investment.

Public investment

Cities must provide public facilities and infrastructure necessary to accommodate development. Where cities are working to encourage redevelopment, they must provide needed public infrastructure. Downtown Greenville was assisted to a great extent by Tax Increment Financing (TIF) in building not only what people consider the traditional public infrastructure but also to provide streetscaping and parking facilities. The concept of Tax Increment Financing is the use of tax revenues generated from new development in a given area to build facilities required to encourage that development. This is done by selling bonds that will be paid back from the incremental additional tax revenues that will come from the development.

Historically, the access to TIF funding is another direct contrast of the two Carolinas. While annexation laws allowed North Carolina cities to gain large areas of land mass and therefore population, they did not have access to TIF Districts, and the cities struggled to have the necessary funds to invest in downtown facilities required to attract redevelopment. This difference was brought home to us in Greenville repeatedly as we hosted North Carolina cities visiting to study the successful downtown development.

With TIF funding, Greenville built a series of strategically placed parking structures to serve development. In some cases, these garages were part of the development, sometimes below the development or in other instances, the development wrapped around the parking structure. The city also did extensive streetscaping. Downtown redevelopment projects can be complex, and it takes a strong public-private partnership to execute them.

Build an active and comfortable core area

In revitalizing a downtown or, for that matter, other areas, there always needs to be a beginning point. There must be an area established not only as a safe zone where people will feel comfortable going but an area with activity that will attract them. That can take many forms such as plazas with nearby active uses. It also helps if the features in the space can help protect people from the harshest aspects of the local weather. From these areas, development can be extended, but there must be a core.

Introducing water into a space can be a great asset. While few places have natural features to build on like the Reedy River Falls, you can introduce water features. Everyone who has been to San Antonio understands the value of the waterway to the Riverwalk tourist area. In Greenville, the River Place development introduced their own terrific waterfall/fountain element. The Main at Broad project also has a wonderful waterwall.

Waterfall at the River Place development

With the deterioration of Downtown Newport News, the city embarked on an effort to create a more centrally located and viable new town center. The city created an attractive and comfortable space with a large water feature with fountains. This is surrounded by office buildings with some retail and restaurants. The office buildings have been very successful. Unfortunately, the space with the fountains is relatively large and there are not sufficient active uses to make the space as active as it could be.

City Center development

When I arrived in Newport News one of the challenges I found for the redevelopment of the area in which Brooks Crossing was located is that they had completed relatively small projects spread throughout the area and no substantial core area was established. This was one of the main reasons I pushed so hard for the Brook Crossing development.

Pedestrian scale design

One's comfort level will be greatly enhanced in a space that has features that are human scale and friendly to pedestrians. This can be done with trees, avoiding tall buildings that are adjacent to plazas, active building facades, public art and street furniture. One of the great design features of Downtown Greenville was a conscious attempt to limit the height of buildings directly fronting on Main Street to four stories or thereabouts and require first floor levels to have active uses and visibility to spaces inside. Along with the pedestrian scaled vegetation, wide sidewalks and protection from cars, the Main Street features space loved by pedestrians.

Typical pedestrian sidewalk streetscaping

Extend core within a comfortable walking distance

Expanding from an active core area is more often successful when it is in increments that are within a comfortable walking distance, generally not much more than a quarter of a mile. This is especially true in hot or cold climates. This was one of the keys to the success the Greenville baseball stadium had in revitalizing the surrounding area.

Event programming

For some places, a major question is how to begin to attract people to an area. Using special events and festivals can provide a great attraction. I believe that the extensive event programming in Greenville was a huge contributor to get people used to coming downtown and enjoying their experience. In fact, this was a significant driver in getting people interested in living downtown. This has led to literally thousands of residences in the central area of the city.

Establish a critical mass of activity

There are lots of ways to activate a space but there needs to be a critical mass that will be enough to draw a crowd. People beget more people. This can be done in a number of ways, but an active use that serves as a draw is important.

Design a space to see and be seen

The design of spaces can help to create a place where people will go to see and be seen. It is human nature to want to interact with others. Creating a place of social interaction is vital to a successful downtown.

Attract different age groups

The most successful downtowns appeal to groups of all ages. When I first arrived in Greenville it was seen as a nice place to raise a family.

However, young people who went away to college were more attracted to go to larger cities like Atlanta, Washington, DC or Charlotte. We designed a specific strategy to appeal to those in their 20s and even 30s. Part of the focus was to create a downtown that would entice them. Driving this was encouraging a live entertainment and bar scene. This was extremely successful and by the end of the first decade of this century Greenville became a hot place to move to for all ages.

Tremendously popular farmer's market in the Ballard neighborhood of Seattle

In fact, the downtown became so attractive to different age groups that it led to some tense times one summer when I was still the manager. Early teens were really attracted to come downtown to be with their friends and meet new people. This became overwhelming when young folks started to use social media to get all their friends to join them downtown. One Saturday night we suddenly had more than 2,000 extra young folks virtually take over downtown. Parents were literally dropping off the teenagers downtown for the evening, virtually as a childcare alternative. We were able to maintain a reasonable environment, but I had to establish a curfew in Falls Park and recommend a city-wide curfew to control the situation.

While these ideas will not guarantee successful downtown development they will certainly give it the best shot to be successful. I have been a student of planning and development for the past five decades and have seen these steps contribute to the success of many cities' revitalization efforts.

The past few chapters have dealt with specific ways to enhance a community. In the next chapter we will shift to working with staff and, in particular, improving the city leadership performance. This brings us to the discussion of the great value of emotional intelligence in enhancing the interpersonal skill of leaders.

Chapter Fifteen

Emotional Intelligence

If I only had one program to institute which would make the biggest difference in an organization, it would be an aggressive program of promoting emotional intelligence. In fact, this is really the only improvement program I instituted in my last three manager stops. There have been many sessions and presentations on emotional intelligence (EQ) at management conferences and seminars. However, I have been surprised that managers have not been more aggressive in establishing effective efforts for their organizations.

The term emotional intelligence was first devised in 1990 by two psychology professors, John D. Mayer and Peter Salovey. I have seen emotional intelligence defined in many ways. In an earlier chapter I described it as the ability to have a clear and true understanding of how others perceive you, to be able to interrelate to others in a positive, constructive manner and to be in control your actions and reactions in given situations, while being true to your own beliefs and not shy away from making contributions as you interact with others.

In 1998, in a key article entitled "What Makes a Leader", published in the Harvard Business Review, Daniel Goleman stated the case for the value of emotional intelligence. He states:

"The most effective leaders are all alike in one crucial way: they all have a high degree of what has come to be known as emotional intelligence. It's not that IQ and technical skills are irrelevant. They do matter, but they are the entry-level requirements for executive positions. My research, along with other recent studies, clearly shows that Emotional Intelligence is the sine qua non of leadership. Without it, a person can have the best training in the world, an incisive, analytical mind, and an endless supply of smart ideas, but he still won't make a great leader." (Daniel Goldman, "What Makes a Leader", *Harvard Business Review*, November-December 1998)

In this article he identifies five key aspects of Emotional Intelligence (descriptions are mine):

- Self-awareness

    This takes into consideration how aware one is about their effect on others, as well as well as how accurately they can interpret how another person is feeling and reacting.

- Self-regulation

    This aspect looks at the ability someone has to be in control of their emotions and reactions in different types of situations, particularly those that are stressful.

- Motivation

  This examines what motivates people beyond money and status. For instance, one would expect local government managers would be motivated to do good beyond just that which would bring them personal gain.

- Empathy for others

  How empathetic people are towards others is measured by this dimension.

- Social skills

  This looks at how proficient one is in managing relationships and building networks.

Moreover, some studies have shown that a person's emotional intelligence is a better indicator of their rise to a leadership position than their IQ. One's ability to be an excellent manager is dependent on their interpersonal relationships. Dealing effectively with stressful situations, being aware of themselves and the reaction of others to them and controlling themselves are all critical to an executive's success.

I have been engaged with emotional intelligence training in a significant way for the past 20 years. My first direct experience was guided by a husband and wife team, John and Athena Miller. I brought them in as consultants when the Executive Director of MAG. They did an amazing job of assisting in the development of a program for the organization and helping me in my own journey to a higher level of emotional intelligence. After my human resources director left the City of Greenville, I recruited Athena Miller to be the new director. Once again in Greenville, Athena and John helped me establish a program for the city leadership. An even more rigorous program that extended the deepest into the management ranks was the effort with the City of Newport News, where over 100 people were engaged.

In each of the three organizations, the EQ programs consisted of three basic parts. First, I have always felt that it was essential to understand the physiological underpinning of how we control (or not, as the case may be) our emotions and responses to given situations. When some people first hear about emotional intelligence, their reaction can be to view it as some psychological mumbo jumbo and dismiss it as some more touchy feely training that will not be very helpful. By better understanding how the body processes situations and develops reactions to them, people can gain more confidence that this is not the latest flavor of the month in training.

The information needs to include an explanation of the various parts of the human brain and how each plays a role in how a person functions and reacts in given situations. This helps people understand how their emotional reactions sometimes can overcome their rational thought and create a response in them which could be out of context with the circumstances. With this knowledge, people can understand how they can control themselves from having an overreaction. It is especially helpful to know the physical signs and signals that can let you know you need to override a potentially inappropriate emotional response.

Say you are in a meeting with a council member and he or she is getting a bit over the top negative about something you have done or not done. One's natural reaction is to rather vigorously defend your position (at least that is my natural reaction!) But if you start to recognize telltale physical reactions to this situation you may be able to head off a less diplomatic response.

The next step was to administer a rigorous EQ instrument to assess each participant's emotional intelligence across a spectrum of dimensions. The most used and tested measure is the EQi 2.0 instrument. Not only has it been extensively tested but I believe it is not as easy to game the system, that is, not respond in a truthful manner but rather how one thinks will look the best. This self-administered assessment provides an amazing amount of information about the emotional intelligence of the person. The feedback is then given to each person by a trained professional. Most people that I have worked with have felt the assessment did an excellent job of describing their EQ. My organizations have had the training on interpreting the assessment results in a group and then in individual sessions with certified professionals.

Knowing the strengths and areas to improve is helpful but it is not really going to make a difference unless there is follow through and, in my opinion, professional coaching. We provided one on one professional coaching. This made all the difference.

If you are not that familiar with EQ and are like many of my department directors, you may be wondering how this makes a difference in the performance of an organization. The first premise is that human interaction is fundamental to everything we do and how that interaction takes place will go a long way in determining the success of any endeavor. More emotionally intelligent team members will have much more positive interaction and more positively support one another. Team performance is greatly enhanced.

Many organizations do not demonstrate that they value individuals. The fact that the EQ program showed that the city cared about each team member was beneficial in and of itself. Even if the EQ worked a lot on an employee's personal issues, including challenges at home, it helped their performance at work.

In order to be more specific about the tangible benefits, I would like to describe how my performance as a manager was enhanced. Early in my management career I was always very businesslike and never really spent a lot of time visiting with staff. I know that some of this was driven by the fact that my first-time full manager position was the Hennepin County Administrator with a very large staff and a very busy schedule. I was working tons of hours and got used to just pressing hard throughout the day. In addition, when in meetings, I would try to get to the point and move through the discussion expeditiously. Due to this way of interacting, some staff did not feel that I really cared about them. In meetings, when I quickly came to understand the presentation and recommendations, some probably did not feel that they had an opportunity to fully explain details they felt were important. I learned to show interest in people and demonstrate that I cared. In addition, I practiced taking time in meetings to give staff feedback; that I understood their presentation, thought process and their recommendations.

The improvement in my relationships with the council and interaction in council meetings was significant due to my EQ training. I learned to be very stoic when council members made crazy statements or got aggressive in their questioning of me or staff. While I had never looked aghast or angry, council members pick up on subtle non-intentional expressions. I knew I got to the point of really mastering this when, my HR Director, Athena Miller, who had coached me in EQ, commented that she did not know how I could sit at the meeting and not react to difficult situations. Always demonstrating respect and deference to the council is important for managers' continued employment.

Emotional intelligence is more than just controlling responses and overreacting, for some it is being more assertive as they tend to defer to others and not feel confident in presenting their ideas. In addition, EQ training can help people understand how they may get reward from their work and even discover if they are well placed in their existing roles in the organization.

This is a summary of some of the key point made in this chapter:

- Emotional intelligence is critical to manager's success

- Training can enhance managers' emotional intelligence

- Emotional intelligence has many dimensions, including ensuring that people are assertive in appropriate situations

- A training program needs to include providing an understanding of EQ, including its physiological basis, use of a rigorous measurement instrument and coaching

- Emotional intelligence needs to be seen as an investment in people that will improve their performance and that of the team as well

As we continue to look at improving organizational performance, the next chapter explores the critically important dimension of performance measurement.

Chapter Sixteen

Outcome Based Performance Measurement

Most all managers would agree that it is important to measure the performance of a city, county of other local government entity. However, what, when and how performance is measured varies widely. Additionally, much time and energy is put into comparing organizations to other similar entities, generally referred to as benchmarking. These efforts are certainly very well intentioned and may provide some useful information; although, I believe the benefits of a great deal of these efforts do not warrant the time and expense required to do the research and produce the reports. For more than 25 years, I have been a strong proponent of outcome based performance measurement. I have sought to exclusively focus on results based measures that can get to the heart of what local governments accomplish for a community.

Managers may feel good about touting that their city paved 100 lane miles of roadways during the past year. So, was that a good thing? Maybe they needed to pave 200 lane miles to keep up with the deteriorating pavement condition. Rather, the measure should be the condition of the roads; isn't that what people care about? Establishing the desired condition for the roadways and measuring whether or not that was achieved seems to me to get to the heart of the matter.

Measuring outcomes or the results of services is not always an easy task. Just to determine the desired result is not easy or straight-forward. And setting a desired level that is reasonable for a community is also complex. For instance, communities may be striving to improve the literacy rate of their citizens. I have seen cities excitedly measure the attendance at libraries or the number of books checked out. While those may both be good things, measuring the literacy rate of citizens is the result that really matters. With limited resources to measure services, cities need to measure what is most important, not just what might be interesting factoids about a library system. The number of books checked out may have very little relationship to building a more literate community if most of the current development of reading skills for people is online.

Focusing on measuring production or output can not only be a waste of time, it will likely not lead the city to better ways of delivering the needed results. For instance, measuring the number of fires extinguished is not getting at what is most important. Rather, measuring the loss of life or injuries caused by fire and the amount of property damage is more important. Putting a fire out after the building has almost burned to the ground is not really a great measure.

Understanding what is important to measure is also difficult when it involves meeting citizen expectations. Crime statistics can be an important measure but citizens feeling safe in their community is also important. Some measures require that citizens be periodically surveyed to determine if services are meeting their expectations.

The outcomes of all types of local government services need to be measured. When I was the Hennepin County Administrator, the Children and Family Services Department was experiencing a major cost overrun for out of home placement. It was so severe that one year the budget was projected to be overspent by several million dollars. Any measure of the amount of money spent or the number of children placed in foster homes would not have shed light on the problem or produced a desirable outcome.

The practice for so many years was totally dysfunctional for the children, basically moving them from one foster home to another until they were 18 with no decision about unification with the parents or processing an adoption. Our focus was on looking at the best outcome for the child. We established a measure that set a goal of either a reunification with the parents or an adoption within six months of the initial separation.

This led the department to examine how best to accomplish that goal. One of the strategies, which proved to be very effective was to send a social worker into the home along with the police when an incident occurred that might result in the child being removed from the home. This gave the social worker a tremendous amount of information about the situation they otherwise would not have had. This was not a common practice 25 years ago. The strategies put in place not only headed off any cost overrun but actually saved money and resulted in timely decisions which greatly improved the lives of the children.

In the City of Newport News we established an Outcome Based Performance Measurement System that included 69 measures which we annually reported at a State of the City presentation. These measures were developed to address the strategic priorities of the city. This provided the city with concrete results-based measures to evaluate services which they paid for. Below is listing of some examples of the measures used:

- Percent of residents working in the city

- Unemployment rate

- Average wage of jobs in the city

- Percent of population below the poverty line

- Average time of approval of site plans

- High School graduation rate

- Percent of college graduates in the city

- Percent of recycled solid waste

- Amount of greenhouse gas reduction

- City streets with at least a satisfactory pavement condition index

- Percent of urban tree canopy

- Percent of residents living within walking distance of a park, accessible open space or trail corridor

- Percent of foster care children obtaining permanency

- Number of identifiable chronically homeless

- Peak travel time along common routes

- Number of Part One crimes

- Monetary value of annual fire loss

- Juvenile detention recidivism rate

- Percent of residents who feel safe in their neighborhood at night

Hopefully, the dimensions of managing a city or county that have been presented in this book are valuable tools that will help managers be successful. However, we all know all does not always work out as a manager would plan and there are times when a manager must part company with their community. We now transition to this challenging situation and how to make the best of it.

Chapter Seventeen

Departing Gracefully

Yes, I am actually writing a chapter on this! How one departs from a local government management position is always important but even more so when the departure is not entirely of your choosing. I believe that most managers work tremendously hard for their community and care deeply about its success. Certainly, there are issues with a manager's performance that cause the council to force out a manager. However, councils also will remove a manager for reasons other than performance. That could be for a personality conflict or could be simply because the council member may be new since the manager was appointed and they want their own person. A council member could feel, rightly or wrongly, that the manager favored the mayor over them or that the manager did not do what the council member wanted.

While it takes at least a majority of council members to vote to remove a manager, it can sometimes only take one or two members that want the manager to be fired to push other council members to vote for removal even if they do not believe the manager should be forced out. Sometimes council members go along just to quiet the dissenters.

While I never having been fired for a performance based issue, according to my councils' comments, I would expect it may be easier to accept if there is indeed a tangible basis to be forced out. I certainly have felt the sting of being pushed out without a performance issue. Of course, I have heard the "management style" comment more than once; coming without any explanation of what that is. So, I am sure you can read in a certain, no significant, no substantial, frustration coming out. It is disheartening to hear that you have done an excellent job as a manager, but the council would like to go in a different direction.

So what do you do when faced with this sort of situation? You suck it up and move on. You knew the rules when you started this game. A council can decide at any time that they would like a new manager. They do not need a reason. It is their absolute right to do so without any reason. You move on and make the best of it. The more that you harbor resentment and anger, the more it will hurt you. This is not about them; it is about you and what you do to be the best manager you can be. Sure, it is difficult, and you want to stay angry, but how much is that going to help? After you ask yourself, "Am I still up for this manager work?", you get over yourself and resolve to be positive. Being fired does not necessarily mean you are a bad person or incompetent or did not do your job. Yes, you should think hard about what you could do differently. However, it does no good to beat yourself up about what happened. Nobody wants to hire someone who is not upbeat and enthusiastic about their work.

I will describe three situations when I was forced to resign; yes, I am afraid, three difficult situations, but all worked out ok. In each of these situations, I signed a separation agreement with the county and two cities that forbids either party from criticizing one another. Thus, my comments will need to be confined generally to public information, although there are some details that do not involve a criticism that will be ok to describe.

El Dorado County

The first position I will describe is the Chief Administrative Officer for El Dorado County, California, which was referenced earlier. This is totally one of those the truth is stranger than fiction stories. All the due diligence I performed did not yield the most important information about the politics of the county. The person from the search firm the county used later apologized for not providing more information about the situation.

The most powerful politician in the county was not one of the board members or the sheriff, but rather the elected county auditor. He approached the status of a political boss of the county. When I applied for the position, two of the five county commissioners were clearly in his camp. Just prior to my interview, a third board member was elected that was also under his influence. As I learned later, he supported me for the position because he believed I was the best candidate. During my first week in the position, he met with me and named six department directors I needed to fire. Furthermore, he informed me, if I did not fire them within the first 30 days, he was going to come out after me. I told him I would be evaluating all the directors to determine if any changes needed to be made in the staffing.

In the first 30 days, I took no action against any of the directors he wanted fired. He was indeed true to his word about coming after me. He tried to trump up issues like the county paying for my mobile phone; imagine that scandal! He was able to make things a bit uncomfortable because his childhood friend was the editor of the local paper. And the editor was married to the treasurer who was also a follower of the auditor. By the way, the county seat is Placerville, also known as "Hang Town" for incidents in it past. Maybe that should have given me a clue!

For the first few months, I was able to hold him at bay with the commission because they liked what I was doing with the organization. However, four months into my tenure, one of the two people on the commission who was not one of the auditor's supporters, got pneumonia, was hospitalized and passed away. Since there was no provision to appoint another member before the regular election many months away, his supporters outnumbered the one remaining commission member he could not influence. They seized the opportunity to force my resignation less than five months into my work with the county. There were no issues or problems, but I was out. Indeed, even if I had not done some good things it would be hard to screw up enough in that time to warrant a forced resignation. However, again, it was their decision.

I negotiated a separation agreement that basically said I would resign and get the severance that was due if I was fired without cause. I spoke nothing about this to the media. The Sacramento Bee, in the county next door castigated the board for their action.

In this situation, it was clear I had not done anything wrong and just needed to move on. I will say, that after it all came out in the wash, it felt like someone was looking out after me. I received 12 months of severance pay which not only helped bridge the gap before I landed my next position as the Greenville City Manager, but I even had a few months left over. I refer to that as my daughters' partial college scholarship money. In addition, when I got the position in California, we had put our home in Arizona on the market. We had lots of people looking but no offers. So when things went south in California, I went back to Arizona and started the search process in earnest. When I landed the position in Greenville, we put our house back on the market. Amazingly, we got on offer from someone who looked at it the first day it was on the market! I am always thankful for being delivered from the very toxic situation it would have continued to be had I stayed!

I will be totally clear, that this was a challenge to put behind me; but it could have been so much worse and looking on the bright side does help. We had found a place in El Dorado we wanted to live. We settled on a house to be built, but the contract we signed was under a contingency that our home needed to be sold. If it had sold and construction had begun on a new home, we would have had to market a home under construction in a place that we were not going to live. All the miles of running came to good use to get beyond this.

City of Greenville

On to the City of Greenville and a match made in heaven, well almost. My wife and I loved Greenville and totally embraced the community and they embraced us. For well over six years, it was a great position and we flourished along with the city. However, during that time most of the city council turned over. The mayor remained and we still are friends, although from a distance. However, there were a couple of newly elected council members who were not supporters. I will not go into that further. They pushed the others for a change. And they all just went along. All the council members but for the two rabble-rousers told me all things were fine with me one day and the next voted in executive session that they wanted me to resign. Council members sometimes tell you what they think you want you to hear, not the truth.

While the mayor was still a supporter, he went along with the two antagonists as it was the path of least resistance. One council member, Amy Ryberg Doyle, did not go along and made her support of me and what I have accomplished very public. She prepared a statement of all that she thought that had been accomplished under my leadership. Despite the peer pressure to just go along, she steadfastly stood up for what she believed in and I will always be most grateful for that.

When the council and I decided I would leave the city manager position and it was announced, a large segment of the community, especially the business community, came unglued. They came to a council work session to berate them. Then there was Father Patrick, the Priest of the church my wife and I attended that picketed city hall wearing a sign protesting the council forcing me out. As unusual as that was, it was also quite touching and special. The newspaper was surprised at my impending departure and

224

tried everything to figure out what the problem was. It was hard to find something that did not exist.

The newspaper presented a difficult dilemma in this process. In their effort to find out what council's concerns might be, they requested a copy of my performance evaluations. While these evaluations were positive, aside from some snippy comments one often gets from an elected body, opening up a manager's personnel evaluations is a slippery slope for setting a precedent. South Carolina law does give the press more leverage for seeing personnel records, but I could have blocked it. However, if I had refused to let them see the evaluations they would have most certainly suspected there was a reason I did not want them public. And they were likely to continue to press for them. I decided to grant them access and would certainly do it again given the same situation. They were still left trying to understand what the problem was.

During the negotiation over a separation agreement, I offered to stay until they could make progress on getting a replacement and to take the city through the budget process. I told them I would work with them without any malice. I remember my words, "I will hold no bitterness in my heart because that will only hurt me". I really believed that is the way I needed to approach it. Again, it was tough and at times, I struggled to keep that promise to myself. When negotiating a separation, a manager obviously needs to look out after their own interest. However, the manager needs to be focused on achieving a fair agreement, not to get even. We agreed upon terms of separation that included me staying on for more than three months. During that three months, you would have thought that no issue existed at all. The council adopted my budget recommendation without changing a penny. They even presented me with a lovely rendering of downtown at my last council meeting. They chose downtown because of all I had done to help its revitalization.

During this time, I worked hard for the city while talking to prospective local private sector employers since my wife and I really wanted to stay in the city. Before I left the city manager position, I had an employment agreement with a private company. That is a story I will tell in the next chapter.

City of Newport News

I hope you are all up for a third story of departure! I will make this short as I have already described the worst chapter in my professional life with the People Express meltdown. While there certainly was some tension between me and at least one or more council members, it was really about each member wanting to control the actions of the city. We had accomplished a lot while I was the manager and they all gave me much of the credit for that. However, the pressure put on the council by the newspaper was more than some council member were willing to take.

Again, in our executive session, I told the council I would totally take the high road and that happened with the separation agreement. Although it was not fully honored by two council members with their public criticism of me, I was not going to take any action on that. We had a most interesting few minutes when we came out of the executive session and I announced my resignation in front of a room packed with media. I thanked the council for the opportunity to serve the city and felt that together we had accomplished some important things. The council was totally unprepared for that and was a bit at a loss for words. However, some expressed thanks as well, and it was an excellent way to go.

One does what they think they should, but you can always have some little self-doubt. I am sure that I could have done some things to improve my performance. But I also know being caught between members on the council was a trap that would have been impossible to avoid. Again, I am so thankful to be out of that situation. I do not regret in any way my time with the city, it was an awesome experience and we got so much done. However, it was tough. I am hopeful that any young manager reading this will not have to go through similar experiences and that many of the more experienced managers have not done so. However, if you do, I hope that my sharing of these experiences will help assist you to get through them and help the experienced manager feel better about things or even grateful they avoided some pain.

I know talking about my experiences have already helped some managers. I have spent a lot of time coaching some prospective city managers who have met with excellent success. I stay in touch with many people I have hired and worked with and provide advice when it is sought. Conversations like one I had with a manager let me know someone is paying attention. I was at a luncheon at a Virginia Local Government Managers Conference several months after leaving the City of Newport News. While talking with a manager, he related to me he had just been forced out of a manager position and wanted to thank me showing him the best way to handle leaving. He said he had watched a video clip from my meeting with the Newport News Council when I resigned and told himself that is the way he would want to go if he was forced out. Indeed, someone was watching.

So, looking back, how do I feel about those three difficult experiences? I go back to Satchel Paige and never looking back. So much good came from my work in Greenville and Newport News and I met people that I will know forever. Maybe this is a bad analogy, but I think of what it must be like for someone who had children from a marriage that ended in a divorce. As painful as that divorce might have been, how can they regret a marriage that brought their children into the world! And, as I reflect on all that was accomplished during my tenure with the places I worked, there was the birth of many wonderful things that help to make those communities better places for the people that live there.

The following are lessons that would be important to remember from the stories in this chapter:

- Always remember it is the council's unilateral right to terminate the manager

- A manager should always take the high road and leave gracefully

- Do what you can to get over the situation and put it behind you

- Learn what you can from the experience

- Do not view a forced separation as indicative of a character flaw, rather be positive about yourself and what you have to offer

- Negotiate a separation agreement that is fair to each party, not to get even with the council

Remember people are paying attention and how you depart will say a lot about your character and professionalism

So what if your answer upon leaving a local government position is that you really do not want to be a manager again. Or, what if you are retiring as a manager yet really want to continue working. I have twice taken the route to move to the private sector after leaving city manager positions. As much as some may have envisioned, it was not a move to the dark side. This is the subject of the next chapter.

Chapter Eighteen

Transitioning to the Private Sector, the Not So Dark Side

My local government management career provided so much reward and allowed me to make many important contributions to communities. While I would not trade that career and experience, I also found my private sector work to be challenging and satisfying. As mentioned in a previous chapter, my Greenville City Manager position and volunteer work exposed me to a wide variety of private firms and businesses. It led to a number of businesses recruiting me. I had seven interviews with companies during the time that I was finishing up with the city.

One of the people who I knew and who approached me to interview with him was Rick Davis, the CEO of Elliott Davis, a relatively large southeast regional accounting firm. The firm had about 450 employees in three states at the time and has since grown to about 800. It was a very deliberative process that led to me taking a position with the firm. We had four meetings, each time focusing in more detail on what I might do with the firm. For the first meeting, I came with my resume and list of skills that I felt would be relevant for the firm. I also included a description of the contacts I had. In addition to the 8,000 names in my Outlook contact file, I had access to more than 75,000 people through the organizations to which I belonged. For the second visit, I developed a role description based on our first conversation. I prepared a relatively detailed job description for the next interview. Finally, for the last meeting, I had developed a six month action plan.

So, after taking a week off after finishing my time with the city, I moved my office four blocks down the road and started with Elliott Davis as the Director of Corporate Development. This was a position created for me. I went from a local government management position with thousands of employees to working for a CEO with only an administrative assistant to supervise. Despite what seems like a major transition, it was totally seamless. To me, so much of what drives success as a local government manager and in my position with Elliott Davis relates to interpersonal skills. Certainly, it helps to have a business sense and perspective. With all the economic development work I had done, that came quite naturally. Of course, managers certainly need to understand financial matters and audits.

While having many different roles with Elliott Davis, one of the most rewarding was establishing an economic development focus for the firm. While the firm had been involved with economic development projects in the past, it was not a significant part of the firm's practice. Rick has always been a CEO who understands market opportunities and avenues to take advantage of them. Leveraging the firm's expertise, especially in International Tax, we positioned the firm to provide services to companies considering relocation to our general market area. By providing initial guidance in their relocation decisions, we were able to gain many additional clients when they made the decision to move. My role included establishing a network of public economic development specialists, attorneys, engineers and others that served as a source for potential firms considering relocation as well as professionals that could help to provide expert advice to the potential clients. This effort helped to grow revenues, particularly for the international practice.

As part of the firm's economic development program, I had the opportunity to join a South Carolina delegation on a business recruitment trip to Israel. Not only was visiting the country a terrific experience but learning about the Israeli entrepreneurial culture was fascinating. In particular, the Israeli acceptance of anyone in an organization questioning current practices has created a culture of innovation which was most instructive.

I spent a productive and enjoyable three years with the firm. During that time, I turned down many recruiters wanting me to be a candidate for city and county manager searches. I never intended to get back into local government management work. However, after accomplishing with the firm most of what I was tasked with doing, the calling to once again be a manager was strong. I have described that next search process already, so I will fast forward to the transition when leaving the City of Newport News.

At that point, my desire to work directly for a city or county council was extinguished. To quote Roberto Duran when he was quitting a title fight repeatedly uttering, "No Mas!" No more, I was and am done; I indeed have said repeatedly. Figuring out the total number of different council members I worked for over 37 years would be virtually impossible but know it must be over 200. Enough for more than one lifetime. However, people know me as a high energy, pretty tireless guy and most people would not have thought I was 65 at the time. I really felt that I had more to give and wanted to continue to make a difference for communities. It seemed that cities and counties could benefit from my experience.

I talked with a number of firms and went through a very similar process with McGill Associates that I had with Elliott Davis. McGill Associates is an engineering and landscape architectural firm headquartered in Asheville North Carolina. I ended up going to work for them as the Director of

Management Services. I was hired to establish a consulting services practice as well as do some business development, training and assist the CEO with new market opportunities. Of course, with my educational training and all the work I had done in my career on capital projects, I felt quite at home working for the firm.

While working on those activities, I was also called upon to lead all the marketing and business development for the firm. We established a significant consulting services practice for the firm, and it was gratifying to assist many communities. While I could have worked with cities and counties on my own as a consultant, I felt that working with a team of professionals with an extensive skill set would enable me to be involved with a more significant impact on communities.

In a twist off irony, as I was winding down my work with McGill, I was approached by Elliott Davis staff about working with them on a proposal to the Metro Nashville Chamber of Commerce to analyze the Metropolitan Nashville and Davidson County budget. This was driven by a concern that the budget of Metro Nashville was in significant stress and they had not taken steps to ensure adequate revenues were available to meet the ever growing needs as the city expanded. I teamed with the Elliott Davis staff and another former City Manager, Gary Jackson, to make the proposal. We were successful in obtaining the work and it was a terrific engagement. Our work was very well received. It was interesting to come back and work on the budget for the place I began my career almost 43 years ago and work with a firm I had left a few years earlier.

To me there are a number of lessons that I would suggest for others looking to make a transition. I suggest the following ideas:

- In the private sector you can still make significant contributions to communities

- While you would still be engaged with councils from time to time, it is a lot different when your livelihood does not depend on them liking what you recommend

- As you approach working for the private sector, think hard about what you like to do and what you could contribute to a firm

- As you would do for a manager position, do your homework; develop a role and job description and then an action plan

- If you are looking at a new position, you need to describe what the result of your work will be, how you will make a difference

Not only is there a great work experience waiting for someone who leaves local government management, but there is much potential reward as well. My experience is that engineers, architects and accountants want to add value and are also very committed to their craft. It isn't the dark side but another opportunity to make a difference.

Chapter Nineteen

So What is Next for You and for Me

Thank you for sharing my journey and a great many of the lessons learned along the way. As everyone knows who makes their way along this path, it is a journey of hard work and some sacrifice. But it is also a journey of great promise and reward. Moreover, it can be a journey of discovery; discovery about the people and communities and those things that are most important to them, discovery about how to make a difference and help make better places and a discovery about yourself and finding meaning in what you do every day.

While I would still like to help people and communities. At this point, it needs to be along different path than managing a city or a county. Writing a book that shares the lessons I learned throughout my career that can hopefully help others is part of that path. I hope that this book will resonate with some that have followed a similar path and they feel a deeply meaningful sense of accomplishment. For those that are on a similar road, my wish is that you can feel the difference you have and will make in communities and be inspired to continue along the path.

I believe managers are driven by an innate, deeply felt desire for service and to help others. We need to celebrate that special trait we share. It needs to give us the strength and courage in those difficult times or when there is a detour in our career path. It needs to give us the confidence to act in the public interest when facing difficult decisions.

After 43 years, I still have a strong desire to help communities and the profession. It is what I wanted to do even before I entered the School of Design at NC State. It is a calling that has driven so many local government professionals for more than a century. While the road is not always easy, would we have it any other way? The bumps along the way will not deter us from seeing what we can accomplish with a great team of people you work with every day.

In assessing a lifetime of being a city/county manager, it seems appropriate to ask if the experience has given more than it has taken. Despite all the myriad of challenges, the rewards outweigh the challenges. If I had to do it all over again, I would be able to make a few mid-course corrections but would go for it once again. The more I reflect on my career, the more I can appreciate the chance to make a meaningful difference.

So where does this leave me? When working as a consultant after leaving the City of Newport News, I met with a manager to introduce our firm to him and his city. I was struck that he said one of the reasons he wanted to meet with me was to see what a manager was like after a long career. He was pleased to see that I was not all shriveled up and barely moving but rather had a lot of energy and enthusiasm. The picture on the next page shows what I looked when serving as the Senior Assistant County Administrator for Hillsborough County. The picture on the page after that is me after serving as a local government CEO for more than twenty years.

However, a manager's life does create changes in you. As a child I always found joy in many things and felt a level of spontaneity in life. That

Picture while serving in as the Senior Assistant County Administrator in Hillsborough County

Picture after serving as a City/County Manager for more than 20 years

level of pure joy and pleasure seemed to be subdued over the many years of demands on my time and anxiety producing circumstances. Until I left being a manager, I did not realize the affect that always being on 24/7 produces. While other professionals say they are on 24/7, it is not the same thing as needing to be ready at literally **any** time night or day for a call that the city has hostage situation or a bomb threat or a major hazardous materials incident.

But this is not a sad story, it has been a good life and we are financially secure for a long retirement. Over the time since I left the City of Newport News, I am feeling a renewed sense of adventure, motivation to do lots of different things and catch up on much that was put aside. That sense of joy and feeling of spontaneity is returning. And, I reflect with great satisfaction on the chance I had to make a demonstrable difference in cities and the lives of the people who live there.

After leaving McGill Associates and reducing my work to some part time consulting, I have had the time to write this book which will hopefully serve the profession. I am actively engaged with our new townhome community, including serving as the president of the homeowner's association. My wife and I have the chance to explore the wonderful Pacific Northwest and travel to different parts of the world. We are enjoying the robust arts and cultural scene in Seattle. Of course, a most important part of our new life is the time with our daughters and granddaughter. As in the past, I also hope to be able to coach other professionals to be successful. This book contains much of the message I want to bring to our professionals.

Ann and I are joined by our granddaughter

So what is next for you? If that is the life of a retired manager, you have earned the right to enjoy yourself and reflect on a life with great meaning and accomplishment. If you are a mid-career professional, please do carry on in the wonderful tradition of public service. If you are just entering the practice of local government management or considering it, go for it. With your eyes wide open and a strong commitment to do good. That is truly what this profession is all about.

Made in the USA
Middletown, DE
18 October 2020